COMEBACK

Also by **DAVID FRUM**

Dead Right

What's Right

How We Got Here: The 70's

An End to Evil

The Right Man

COMEBACK
Conservatism That Can Win Again

David Frum

DOUBLEDAY

<small>New York London Toronto Sydney Auckland</small>

PUBLISHED BY DOUBLEDAY

Copyright © 2008 by David Frum

All Rights Reserved

Published in the United States by Doubleday, an imprint of The Doubleday
Broadway Publishing Group, a division of Random House, Inc., New York.

www.doubleday.com

DOUBLEDAY and the portrayal of an anchor with a dolphin are registered trademarks
of Random House, Inc.

Book design by Fearn Cutler de Vicq

Library of Congress Cataloging-in-Publication Data

Frum, David, 1960–

Comeback : conservatism that can win again / David Frum. — 1st ed.

p. cm.

Includes bibliographical references and index.

1. Conservatism—United States. 2. Republican Party (U.S.: 1854–).
3. United States—Politics and government—2001– I. Title.

JC573.2.U6F75 2007

320.520973—dc22

2007034787

ISBN 978-0-385-51533-7

PRINTED IN THE UNITED STATES OF AMERICA

1 3 5 7 9 10 8 6 4 2

First Edition

To Peter Worthington,
Who Taught Courage to Three Generations

CONTENTS

COMEBACK

GEORGE W. BUSH:
What Went Wrong?

In January 2003, I published one of the very first memoirs of the Bush administration, *The Right Man: The Surprise Presidency of George W. Bush.*

Over the years since, the Bush administration has been hammered by difficulties and disappointments. And I have often found myself fighting against the administration I once served: against the prescription drug plan, against the Harriet Miers nomination to the Supreme Court, against amnesty for illegal aliens. During those fights, it was usually only a matter of time before I was sarcastically asked, "So—is George Bush still 'the right man'?"

On the credit side: George Bush led the U.S. economy through its longest-ever expansion. He correctly identified the tyranny and misgovernment of the Middle East as the crucial cause of Islamic terrorism. He enhanced the security of the whole world by removing Saddam Hussein from control of the second most important Arab oil state. Bush showed courage on stem cells, and (Miers aside) he nominated excellent conservative judges.

On the debit side: So many mistakes! And such stubborn refusal to correct them when there was still time! So many lives needlessly sacrificed, so much money wasted, so many friends alienated, so many enemies strengthened. No American president since Harry Truman has been so unpopular so long as George W. Bush. Bush's Republicans suffered one fearful defeat in 2006 and seem poised to suffer another in 2008. A generation of young Americans has been lost to our party.

What went wrong? Many will want to load the blame for all the disappointments of the Bush presidency on the president himself. He surely deserves much of the blame. Why did he appoint such consistently mediocre people to such important jobs? Where was he in the summer of 2003, as Iraq began to go wrong? Why did he keep saying one thing and then doing the opposite on issues from Middle Eastern democracy to the North Korean nuclear bomb? Why did he make so little effort to persuade the American public? Why defy the nation and the party and adopt immigration amnesty as a supreme priority? Why did he spend so lavishly—while improving government so little?

I warned in 2003 of George Bush's stubbornness, his hastiness, and his inattention to detail. I believed then that his sheer determination to prevail in the war on terror would elevate him above such limitations. In that belief I was mistaken. Bush's eagerness for bold action was again and again frustrated by his disinclination to acknowledge unwelcome realities. He persuaded himself that the regimes most responsible for the growth of radicalism—Saudi Arabia and Pakistan—could nonetheless be relied upon as allies. He publicly declared that he would prevent Iran from acquiring nuclear weapons, without any strategy to make his word good. In his eagerness to avoid condemning all Muslims as terrorists, he deceived himself about the prevalence of extremism among Muslims world-wide. George W. Bush had the right instincts, but the wrong methods. He identified the right path, but stumbled when he tried to walk it.

Yet we conservatives and Republicans must face some truths about ourselves as well. In important ways, Bush saw more clearly than we. He recognized that the conservatism of the 1980s and 1990s had exhausted itself.

After the triumph of 1994, we lost the battle over the government shutdown in 1995. Running as a Reagan conservative, Bob Dole lost the presidential election of 1996. In the court of public opinion, we lost the impeachment fight. We lost the congressional elections of 1998—the first time since 1822 that a non–presidential party had failed to gain seats in the sixth year of a presidential term.

Bush had won the biggest Republican victory of that otherwise frustrating year. He was reelected governor of Texas in 1998 by the highest margin of any reelected governor in the country, almost 70 percent of the vote, due in large measure to his breakthrough success among women and minorities.

Republicans turned to George Bush because he seemed to offer an escape from a dead end into which we had steered ourselves. Had we nominated a Reagan-style conservative in 2000, we would certainly have lost again. Bill Clinton left office tainted by scandal—but protected by a 65 percent end-of-presidency approval rating, higher than Reagan's, higher than Eisenhower's.

The 2000 election could easily have proven itself a 1988 in reverse. Al Gore could have won a third Clinton term just as George H. W. Bush won a third Reagan term. If the Republicans had nominated a principled small-government conservative in 2000, Gore surely *would* have won that third term. Instead, it was George W. Bush who cunningly presented himself as Clinton's true heir. Like Clinton, Bush vowed to protect Medicare and Medicaid from all proposals to retrench or reform them. Like Clinton, Bush claimed a record as an "education governor." Like Clinton, Bush promised a small tax cut only after he had met all his spending priorities. Like Clinton, Bush deftly maneuvered his opponents away from the political center. By Election Day 2000, it was Gore who was running as the candidate of change ("the people versus the powerful"); it was George W. Bush who was promising to continue the Clinton prosperity without the Clinton scandals.

Bush often told aides that his top political priority was to "change the party," that is, to move it away from the Reagan-style conservatism of the 1980s toward a new, softer centrism. His party, however, believed that he was leading the nation back toward Reagan-style conservatism. This obvious contradiction placed Bush in a terrible bind from the very start. His failure to win a popular-vote mandate in November 2000 tightened the bind. Bush sought to escape his dilemma through a careful balancing of policies, sometimes leaning left, sometimes right—again mimicking the Clinton model.

Triangulation worked for Clinton because he ceased after 1994 to try to do anything big. Clinton ran his presidency in survival mode, avoiding risks, minimizing his political vulnerabilities. Bush, however, hated "small ball." He took big risks, but he took those risks for the sake of policies radically at odds with one another.

In the war on terror, Bush triangulated between promoting democracy to defeat Islamism and supporting authoritarian allies against Islamism. He sought to defeat radical Islam with the support of radical Islam's principal backers: the Saudi monarchy and the Pakistani military. He ended up running two contradictory foreign policies, and unsurprisingly, both ended badly.

At home, Bush triangulated between radical free-market reforms in Social Security and Medicare on the one hand and a huge expansion in government's grip upon prescription drugs, farming, and energy on the other. He cut taxes and increased spending. He sought to protect the nation from foreign terrorists while propping open the doors to huge new waves of foreign immigration. Unsurprisingly, these contradictory policies ended badly too.

Presidential reputations fluctuate over time. Harry Truman left office reviled as a cheap, small-time huckster, a man of intemperate language who had stumbled into a vicious, costly, and inconclusive war in Korea, while presiding over inflation and corruption scandals at home. Dwight Eisenhower was ridiculed as an inarticulate dunce manipulated by an all-powerful secretary of state. Not until the 1960s did Truman get credit for his achievements; not until the 1980s did historians obtain access to the presidential papers that demonstrated that Ike always gave the orders. By contrast, the reputation of President Kennedy has tended to decline since his assassination, and Richard Nixon's has never recovered from his resignation.

What judgment will future generations render upon George W. Bush? I hope and believe it will be a positive one, but I will predict only that neither the country nor the party can or will revert to the policies that prevailed before Bush. Not to Clintonism, because Clinton's passivity and complacency in the 1990s left the country vulnerable to the catastrophe of 9/11. And not to Reaganism, because Reagan Republicanism offers solutions to the problems of forty years before, not to those of the twenty-first century. Both the country and the party have to work their way forward from the Bush experience, not back to some mythical golden past.

I began work on this book at the apogee of George Bush's success, in the weeks after the 2004 election. Those were days of Republican triumphalism and Democratic dismay. "Republican hegemony in America is now expected to last for years, maybe decades," the conservative journalist Fred Barnes exulted soon after the 2004 vote.[1] Al From of the Democratic Leadership Council lamented that his party had suffered "a 40-year slide which we interrupted a little bit during the '90s, but it has resumed with the 2000 and 2002, 2004 election. . . . This slide is not going to stop on its own."[2]

That all looks absurd now. But evidence abounded that it was wrong even in 2004. Bush won reelection that year by just two percentage points of the popular vote: a narrower margin of victory than that of any reelected president in U.S. history. The campaign itself had been a terrifying and terrible experience, with Bush delivering in the first presidential debate one of the worst performances of his entire political career. (Early in the debate, Bush boasted that bin Laden had been "isolated." I flinched when I heard this, awaiting the "You're no Jack Kennedy" killer comeback: "Isolated? Isolated? Why isn't the son of a bitch *dead*?!" Fortunately, John Kerry never used language like that—too judgmental.)

The American public had been trending leftward on economic and cultural issues since the middle 1990s. The shock of 9/11 halted the drift in 2002 and again in 2004. But if Republicans looked beyond the headlines, they had every reason to worry that the drift would resume as soon as the memory of 9/11 faded.

- The American economy grew handsomely between 2001 and 2006. But over those five years, the income of the median American— the worker right in the middle of the pay scale—did not rise at all. The number of people in poverty rose by 5.4 million between 2000 and 2004.

- The 9/11 attacks exposed terrifying unreadiness throughout the U.S. government. In response, the Bush administration launched the most radical overhaul of the U.S. government since the beginning of the Cold War—only to be caught almost equally unprepared by Hurricane Katrina.

- Between 2001 and 2006, at a time of intense concern for national security, at least 4 million people entered the United States illegally, elevating the total illegal population to at least 12 million.

- For the first time in half a century, Republicans controlled the presidency, the House, and the Senate all at the same time. Instead of rolling back government, however, we hugely expanded it. Federal spending under George W. Bush rose faster than under any president since Lyndon Johnson.

- In his 2002 State of the Union speech, President Bush pledged to prevent the world's most dangerous regimes—he named Iraq, Iran, and North Korea—from acquiring nuclear weapons. Five years later, North Korea had tested a nuclear bomb and Iran looked likely to follow soon.

- Republicans won in 1994 and 2000 due in large part to voter perceptions of them as the more honest and ethical party.[3] This asset was squandered by Jack Abramoff, Duke Cunningham, Mark Foley, and Alberto Gonzalez.

More than most presidents, George W. Bush has left behind a mixed record: of work begun but left unfinished, of challenges confronted but ill articulated, of heroic aspirations marred by ineffective execution, of bold initiatives and tentative results.

Sometimes I ask myself: What would have happened if George W. Bush had lost the election of 2004? That, I still feel sure, would have been an unmitigated catastrophe for the United States. Here is how some of John Kerry's staunchest supporters described the man who would have replaced George Bush in the Oval Office: "the least appealing candidate the Democrats have nominated for president in my lifetime. . . . He's pompous, he's an opportunist, and he's indecisive."[4] A Bush defeat in 2004 would have been interpreted worldwide as a collapse of American nerve, a repudiation of the very idea of a strong response to terrorism. Had Bush lost that year, the Republican Party would have been surprised, shocked, shattered, and might well have gone veering off into isolationism or recoiling backward to the country club politics of the elder George Bush.

At other times I wonder: What would have happened if Bush had failed to prevail in 2000? That is a harder question to answer. Had Al Gore won that year, he would have been constrained by a Republican Congress. No Supreme Court vacancies opened in the 2001–2005 term. Instead of John Kerry attacking Bush's war on terror from the left, the 2004 election would probably have seen Republicans nominating Rudy Giuliani to critique Al Gore's response to 9/11 from the right. Perhaps then 2004 would have been the year that the elusive majority Republicans have been seeking since 1990 would finally have consolidated itself. Who can say?

But we can say this: In 2000, Bush won a victory that probably no other Republican could have won. By 2008, he had led his party to the brink of disaster.

George Bush's party now looks beyond George Bush. The contest to elect the next Republican president began astonishingly early. It may continue for a dismayingly long time. That next president will need wisdom, courage, patience, and principle. He will also need a new generation of ideas. This book represents one Bush veteran's vision of what those ideas might be.

WHY WE'RE LOSING

By the final months of the Bush presidency, nearly two-thirds of Americans had concluded that the Iraq war was a mistake. Almost three-quarters believed that the country was on the "wrong track," an astonishingly bad number for a nonrecession year.

Large majorities of Americans preferred Democrats to Republicans on virtually every public policy issue. Americans regarded Democrats as more competent by a margin of 5 to 3, more ethical by a margin of 2 to 1. They credited Democrats as caring more about "people like them." Americans even preferred Democrats on taxes.

On the day they reelected President Bush in 2004, equal numbers of Americans identified themselves as Republicans and Democrats. By 2007, Democrats outnumbered Republicans 3 to 2. The generation of Americans that turned twenty between 2000 and 2005 identified with the Democrats by the largest majority recorded for any age cohort since modern polling began after World War II.

Since 2003, the once formidable Republican advantage in fundraising has collapsed. Democratic Internet sites draw more traffic and more enthusiasm than anything Republicans or conservatives can offer. Republicans are dispirited and demobilized; Democrats, united and galvanized.

Republicans offered Americans an array of capable and experienced candidates in the 2008 presidential cycle; Democrats, two neophytes and a former first lady. Yet as the 2008 election cycle commenced, almost every one of these miserably weak Democrats beat almost every one of these impressive Republicans in head-to-head poll matchups.

Conservatives were brought to power in the 1970s and 1980s by liberal failure. Now conservative failure threatens to inaugurate a new era of liberalism. Rather than take the measure of our troubles, however, we are denying them. Rather than adapting to new times, we are indulging ourselves in nostalgia for past successes.

Ronald Reagan campaigned in 1980 on a promise to cut income-tax rates. He won decisively. Since then, two other Republicans have campaigned on a similar promise: Bob Dole in 1996 and George W. Bush in 2000. In both elections, polls consistently indicated that the public preferred deficit reduction to tax cuts. Republicans simply refused to believe it. One leading consultant told me in 1996 that no matter what people said about tax cuts, they would always vote for them: "We're leaving a wrapped candy bar in the privacy of the polling booth—and when the voter steps out, there will be an empty wrapper on the floor." It did not happen that way, and for reasons that could have been predicted.

When Republicans speak of "tax cuts," they mean "income tax cuts." Yet after almost three decades of income-tax cutting, most Americans no longer pay very much income tax. In fact, four out of five taxpayers now pay more in payroll taxes than federal income taxes. Some 29 million income-earning American households pay no income tax at all.[1] By contrast, the notorious top 1 percent of taxpayers pay well over one-third of all U.S. income taxes. The top

1 percent may make a disproportionate amount of money. But they still cast only 1 percent of the votes.

Conservative success has likewise retired the crime issue. In the single year 1974, one out of every three American families suffered a serious crime. Victimized and frightened, voters rated crime the single most important issue facing the country. Between 1990 and 2000, the American crime rate plunged—and by 2006, crime had dropped to ninth place on the Harris poll's list of public concerns, after terrorism/national security, the economy/jobs, energy prices, health care, education, the environment, Social Security, and poverty.[2]

Hmm, how about inflation? Americans grumble about the cost of living. It showed up in many polls as an important issue in 2005. But inflation in the 1970s sense—a general increase in the price level—has dwindled almost to nothing. The cost increases Americans struggle with today trace either to swings in the price of highly variable commodities (oil, gas, food) or else to a few key markets badly distorted by government subsidy and intervention (housing, health care, and college tuition). In either case, however, the monetarist policies used to halt the inflation of the 1970s can do little to help.

Public disgust with welfare drove voters to the GOP in 1994. Welfare costs are now rising again. This time, it is Republicans, not Democrats, who are responsible. In 2001, President Bush and the Republican Congress restored immigrant eligibility for social welfare programs. Over the next five years, enrollment in the food stamp program alone jumped by 9 million people.[3]

It's not just the issues that have changed. The country is changing, and in ways deeply inhospitable to the Republican Party.

The Republicans draw their strength from white America, the Democrats from nonwhite America. European Americans are rapidly dwindling: from 80 percent of the population in 1980 to 70 percent in 2000, and then (if current trends continue) to probably a hair over 60 percent by 2020.

Married women vote Republican, unmarried women vote Democratic. The number of women who had not married by their late thirties doubled between 1980 and 2000.

Parents vote Republican, the childless vote Democratic. Between 1980 and 2000, the number of women who had not given birth by age forty also doubled.

Churchgoers vote Republican, the secular vote Democratic. While church attendance is notoriously difficult to measure, it does seem to have declined sharply since 1970: By 2000, probably at least one-quarter of Americans rarely or never attended church. Almost 15 percent of Americans describe themselves as "without religion."[4]

The moderately educated vote Republican, while both the highly educated and the uneducated vote Democratic. Between 1980 and 2000, the proportion of Americans with graduate degrees shot up from too few for the Census Bureau to count to almost 9 percent of the population. Meanwhile, barely half of the rapidly growing minority population is graduating from high school.[5]

Where you see a white, married, middle-class, middle-aged church-going family with children there you probably behold Republican voters. Where church attendance is high and military vocations are popular, Republicans are strong. If you finished college but not graduate school, if you earn more than $75,000 but less than $200,000, you probably belong to the great Republican middle. The more emphatically you agree that people who work hard can get ahead; that the rules are basically fair; that you are "extremely proud" to be an American—the more likely you are to vote for the Grand Old Party.

And it is precisely this great American middle that is shrinking before our eyes.

After the disturbing elections of 1996 and 2000, the great political observer Michael Barone tried to cheer up Republicans by pointing out that Red State America had more children than Blue State America. Conservatives might be ceasing to outvote liberals—but they were at least outbreeding them! Similarly, Phillip Longman, a liberal writer interested in demography, worried after the 2004 election that the average fertility rate in states that voted for George Bush was more than 11 percent higher than the rate in states that voted for John Kerry.[6]

But this is the very opposite of good news for Republicans. The reason that the red states have so many more children than the blue states is that they have so many more Hispanic immigrants. And those increasing Hispanic populations will slowly but surely push red states into the blue column.

Look at California, once a Republican bastion. California voted for Nixon over Kennedy in 1960 and Ford over Carter in 1976. Since 2000, California has become a majority-minority state—and a Democratic bastion. As things are going, Florida, Colorado, and even Texas will likely follow.

Texas tipped majority-minority in 2006. As yet, very few Texas Hispanics have acquired the right to vote. One-third of Texas Hispanics are noncitizens. Almost half of Texas's citizen Hispanics are younger than age eighteen, so they cannot vote either. If those noncitizens are legalized and naturalized—when those under-eighteens grow up—Texas will likely trend Democratic.

Many of us on the right would like to believe that Republicans got into trouble by abandoning conservative principle. I'd like to believe it myself. The evidence, unfortunately, does not support that view. On the contrary, the evidence suggests that a more consistent, more principled, more conservative administration would have been even more soundly rejected by the public than the unpopular Bush administration ever was:

- Conservatives worry that Bush spent too much and cut taxes too little. But most Americans wanted the federal government to spend more rather than tax less. By margins of more than 5 to 4, Americans condemn the Bush tax cuts as "not worth it."[7] When offered a clear choice between cutting taxes or balancing the budget during election year 2004, Americans opted for budget balancing by a margin of 2 to 1. When the choice was changed to cutting taxes or increasing spending, they opted for higher spending by a margin of 5 to 4.[8] During the second Clinton term, more than 60 percent of Americans complained that their personal tax burden was "too high." Since 2001, that figure has dropped below 50 percent.[9]

- Conservatives (me too) condemned Bush for adding a prescription drug benefit to Medicare without obtaining cost-cutting reforms in return. But public support for the benefit ranged between 80 percent and 90 percent through the first Bush term.[10] Even when warned that the benefit might cost more than $400 billion over the next decade, support diminished only slightly, to about 75 percent.[11] Had Bush heeded conservative advice on this issue, he would very likely have lost the 2004 election.

- Conservatives dislike Bush's No Child Left Behind education reforms. We would have preferred reforms that promoted school choice, held failing schools to account, and reduced federal education spending. A misguided public firmly rejects all these conservatives views. When asked, "Should we close poorly performing schools?" 77 percent of Americans said "no." When asked, what should be done instead with these bad schools, 77 percent of Americans answer: Give them more money. What about firing bad principals or teachers? Americans support that idea, but by surprisingly narrow margins: 56–40. Consistently, between 60 percent and 70 percent of Americans reject the idea of shifting from the existing public school system to some new alternative.[12]

- Conservatives favor a muscular approach to terrorism and quietly worry that the second-term George Bush has been too weak. Most Americans, however, take an increasingly skeptical view of military action. Between 2002 and 2006, the proportion of Americans who thought military force could reduce the risk of terrorism dropped by 16 points, from 48 percent to 32 percent.[13]

- Conservatives staunchly backed President Bush's bold stance against federal aid to embryo-killing stem-cell research. Yet a consistent majority of Americans surveyed opposes the president's stand, even when the poll question carefully explains that this research destroys potential human life.[14]

- Many conservative constitutionalists resent President Bush's decision to sign the McCain-Feingold campaign finance reform, despite the president's own previously expressed opinion that the bill violated the Constitution. Few Americans—under 10 percent—take any serious interest in campaign-finance reform, and so a veto would probably have been politically cost-free. On the other hand, the preferred conservative reform—lift campaign limits so long as the source of the money is disclosed—is opposed by more than 75 percent of Americans.[15]

On issues from Social Security to health care to environmental protection, conservatives find themselves on the less popular side of the great issues of the day. That does not mean that conservatives are wrong. But it does mean that we are likely to lose if we continue repeating old formulas without adapting them to new times.

The last of the New Deal politicians, House Speaker Tip O'Neill, used to complain bitterly about the ingratitude of the American voter. The Democrats, O'Neill said, had created the American middle class—and now that middle class was voting Republican. It seems never to have occurred to O'Neill that a prosperous middle-class nation might need or want different policies from the Depression-battered society in which he grew up. As O'Neill saw it, what was right for 1937 was just what was required in 1977.

Are we conservatives and Republicans repeating O'Neill's mistake?

In the Republican debates of 2007, candidate after candidate invoked the name and memory of Ronald Reagan. I wish a candidate had said: Ronald Reagan was a good man and a great president. What made him great was his ability to respond to the demands of his times. We must respond to the demands of ours.

When Ronald Reagan ran for president against Gerald Ford in 1976, the federal government set the price of oil and natural gas. It regulated airfares, truck routes, and train schedules. It controlled the interest rate paid on checking accounts and the fees charged by stockbrokers. It had only just recently legalized the private ownership of gold. It decided who was—and who was not—allowed to broadcast on radio and television, and it closely monitored the format and content of what they said. Federal judges ran school districts, busing children hither and yon in pursuit of racial balance. The marginal income-tax rate for a typical middle-class family of four almost doubled between 1968 and 1980, even as that family's standard of living stagnated or declined.

In such a world, Ronald Reagan's promises to restore freedom by curtailing government powerfully resonated.

Between 1968 and 1980, the United States suffered a series of serious geopolitical defeats. It lost a war in Indochina and endured an oil boycott by OPEC. Soviet-backed insurgents seized power in Central America. America's most important ally in the Persian Gulf, the Shah of Iran, was toppled by revolution. The Soviet nuclear arsenal equaled and exceeded that of the United States, and Soviet-supported terrorist movements waged war against the governments of Italy, West Germany, Israel, and the United Kingdom. In 1979,

Soviet troops invaded Afghanistan, the first large Soviet deployment outside its accepted zone of influence since the Cuban Missile Crisis.

Against such threats, Reagan's strength and optimism met the challenge of the times.

But now?

If there is anything that George Bush has not lacked, it is the spirit of optimism. He bet his presidency on a sequence of best-case scenarios, headed by the gamble that Iraq could be subdued with half the number of troops estimated by the Pentagon. Nor does America lack strength. The world's only superpower has never been stronger. What haunts Americans is doubt that the nation's strength has been used intelligently. It is more brains, not more brawn, that Americans want from their next administration.

And while many of the country's most pressing domestic problems can be traced to government—the health insurance problem is horribly aggravated by perverse tax incentives—few of them can be fixed by Reagan-style tax cutting and deregulation. The energy market is already mostly deregulated. Ditto the mortgage market. More generally, how many Americans in these opening years of the twenty-first century feel too little liberty to do what they want to do? When Ronald Reagan warned in 1964 against the anthill society of communism, he was warning against something vivid and real: The very next year, the world's most populous society would be plunged into a "cultural revolution" in which the society's leaders would try to extinguish human individuality by abolishing names and replacing them with numbers. When Reagan in that same great speech invoked the maximum of human liberty consistent with social order, he spoke at a time when order seemed abundant and liberty in short supply. The draft still existed in 1964. Today, our whole planet is seething with human dynamism—and the worries politicians hear on front steps are worries about disorder: illegal drugs, uncontrolled migration, and income volatility.

If Republican politicians quote Reagan, their political operatives study Nixon. It was Richard Nixon who discovered that middle-class Americans despised arrogant and permissive social elites much more than they resented wealthy economic elites. Republicans have been reprising Nixon's 1972 campaign against McGovern for a third of a century. As the excesses of the 1960s have dwindled into history, however, the 1972 campaign has worked less and less well. Four decades after Appomattox, even the Grand Old Party of Lincoln and Grant recognized that it could no longer win votes by waving the bloody shirt. FDR's party eventually accepted that nobody remembered Herbert Hoover anymore. How many more elections can conservatives win by campaigning against Abbie Hoffman and Bobby Seale?

Voters want solutions to the problems of today, and those are the solutions that today's conservatives have to invent and develop. There's a marvelous story from the 1950s about an ex-Communist who got into an argument with a young man newly infatuated with Marxism. The older man retorted: "Your answers are so old that I've forgotten the questions."

If we conservatives and Republicans want to win again, we have to offer the American voter something fresh and compelling—answers to the problems of today, not the problems of the era when disco ruled. Ronald Reagan was elected at a time when every social indicator seemed to be moving in the wrong direction. Ronald Reagan's optimism refreshed the country because so many Americans had lost hope in their society. Today, Americans worry less about their society than about the competence and effectiveness of their government. Our conservative and Republican failures have fed those worries.

In the heady days of 1994, some conservatives joked about shrinking government to a size small enough to drown in a bathtub. That did not sound so amusing after we witnessed New Orleans drowned in a hurricane. There are things only government can do, and if we conservatives wish to be entrusted with the management of the government, we must prove that we care enough about government to manage it well.

The most dangerous legacy Reagan bequeathed his party was his legacy of cheerful indifference to detail. Yes, it worked for him. It worked for John F. Kennedy to run the presidency buzzed on painkillers. Kennedy's ability to beat the odds is not a model to be emulated, and neither is Reagan's. The next Republican president needs to master details, understand his options, and make his decisions with care.

Americans are asking new questions. Conservatives who aspire to govern America had better provide new answers.

THREE

HOW WE WIN

I t was Bill Clinton of all people who pointed out to us what that new conservative answer should be. In a pensive moment late in 1997, President Clinton observed: "There are a lot of very brilliant people who believe that the nation-state is fast becoming a relic of the past."[1] He was right: A lot of people, brilliant and not so brilliant, do believe that. Republicans and conservatives do not. And it is this disagreement that increasingly defines the difference between the parties.

Democrats are consistently less likely than Republicans to describe themselves as "extremely proud" to be Americans. As of January 2005, for example, 71 percent of Republicans described themselves as "extremely proud," but only 54 percent of Democrats did.[2] On the eve of the Iraq war in March 2003, 72 percent of Republican high-school seniors described themselves as "very" or "extremely" patriotic, while only 41 percent of Democratic high-school seniors did so.[3]

Liberals and Democrats believe in government. They put much

less trust in the people who elect that government. Democrats are consistently less likely than Republicans to express confidence in the ability of the United States to solve its problems, a gap that widened to an astonishing 13 points in 2003 and then to a record 19 points in 2007. Democratic voters are much more likely to attribute success or failure in life to forces beyond individual control, and to express pessimism and passivity in the face of personal adversity.[4] Believing in government, but lacking faith in America and Americans, Democrats are naturally attracted to institutions of global governance. Mistrusting traditional American culture as racist, violent, and generally defective, Democrats bring little enthusiasm and less perseverance to that culture's defense.

So it is we Republicans and conservatives who are called on to defend America and Americans. Back in the 1990s, my friend David Brooks proposed a politics of "national greatness." Brooks never quite got around to explicating what he meant—indeed, with characteristic whimsy, he suggested that the contents of such a politics "almost didn't matter."[5]

Brooks could be so lighthearted because the politics of the 1990s were so trivial and the dangers surrounding the nation so hidden from view. A decade later, things look grimmer. America's rivals are gaining, America's friends are declining, and America's cohesion in a time of danger is threatened by divisions of culture, race, language, and class.

Americans are trapped in obsolete politics, engaging in phony arguments over issues that are in fact largely settled. Political partisans fail to learn from their opponents even when they discover something new and true. As people gain affluence, additional increments of money come to matter less—and nonmaterial aspects of life come to matter more. That is the fundamental and almost inherent reason that environmentalism has come to loom so large in the politics of advanced democracies, and yet we as Republicans and conservatives seem almost paralyzed to accept this palpable fact. We see consumers voluntarily choosing to pay more for higher-quality food. Why should we be surprised that some will choose to pay more for cleaner energy? Yet we Republicans treat the coal industry with the same protective reverence that Democrats grant to their school-destroying allies in the teachers' unions.

The battle between capitalism and socialism is over. Capitalism won. The battles raging now are battles over the future of the nation in a world in which new forms of identity seek to overpower the nation from above and divide it from below.

Corrode national sovereignty and you corrode democracy. No individual person votes for the UN Secretary-General or the European Commissioners. No legislature writes the laws enforced by the International Criminal Court. A decade ago, Tony Blair's adviser Alister Campbell observed the growth of such international bodies and predicted that the era of representative democracy was drawing to a close. A shrewd remark. There can be no global democracy until there is a global electorate. Lacking a global electorate, global governance must be nondemocratic governance.

When we conservatives and Republicans define our politics as the politics of American nationhood, we champion not only this nation, but all nations. We champion not only nationhood, but democracy.

Democrats and Republicans are replicating a political battle waged throughout the advanced industrial world. Should democratic societies organize themselves as "nations" with a single language and a shared culture? Or does the future belong to multinational governing institutions like the European Union and the United Nations? Is diversity always a strength? Or can excessive diversity ultimately undermine the social trust and mutual accommodation on which democracy rests?

Many on the left yearn to build new structures of international governance: the Kyoto Accord, an international criminal court, an aggrandized UN Security Council. These new institutions differ radically from the institutions created after 1945: NATO, the old General Agreement on Tariffs and Trade, the Organization for Economic Cooperation and Development, the International Monetary Fund. The post-1945 institutions were created to enhance the effectiveness of nations, to provide greater military and economic security to their populations, to support and enhance democracy. The new globalism, by contrast, aims not to strengthen nations, but to subordinate them; not to consolidate democracy, but to constrain it.

There is a big difference between a free-trade agreement by which a government undertakes not to discriminate against foreign firms—and a Kyoto Accord, which grants a multinational organization power to regulate the business operations of domestic firms. There is a big difference between a NATO alliance, by which a group of democratic nations pledge to come to each other's defense—and Kofi Annan's claim that a war is illegal unless approved by a UN Security Council on which two nondemocratic nations wield vetoes. There is a big difference between the market-opening European Economic Community of the 1960s—and the determination of the new European Union to place voter-constraining power over such issues as taxes, war, and peace in the hands of an unelected commission in Brussels. There is a big difference between America signing the Universal Declaration of Human Rights defining the moral standard that all governments must meet if they wish to be considered civilized—and congressional Democrats pushing to join an international criminal court that would subject Americans to criminal prosecution by an international body devoid of the protections guaranteed by the U.S. Constitution. There is a big difference between the U.S. Senate ratifying treaties to promote U.S. interests—and justices on the U.S. Supreme Court using their power to interpret American law to incorporate treaties the Senate has declined to ratify.[6]

These are the great debates of our time, and they divide Americans much more than debates over the proper role of trade unions or the acceptable top rate of income tax. The hottest of hot-button issues in early-twenty-first-century America are the issues that challenge Americans to define what it means to be an American: immigration, affirmative action, bilingualism, national sovereignty, community loyalty, and the role of the United States in the world.

More than one in nine residents of the United States were born abroad. This large population comes overwhelmingly from a single foreign country, Mexico. They speak a single language and are concentrated in a region of the country, the Southwest, to which their homeland has irredentist claims. Court rulings since the 1970s have conferred quasi-official status on the Spanish language in American schooling and balloting. The mechanisms by which past waves of migration were assimilated have either (like the draft) vanished or else (like the public schools) abandoned their former mission. So weak is the assimilationist ideal that the two most visible American Muslim groups felt emboldened to condemn the Afghanistan war barely six weeks after the 9/11 attacks.

Over the decades, Republicans have been many things: the party of the Union, the party of the gold standard, the party of temperance, the party of free enterprise, and the pro-life party, among others. Amid all these changes, there is one thing that has never changed: Republicans have always been the party of American democratic nationhood.

Democrats, by contrast, have historically tended to attract those who felt themselves in some way marginal to the American experience: slaveholders, indebted farmers, immigrants, intellectuals, Catholics, Jews, blacks, feminists, gays—people who identify with the "pluribus" in the nation's motto, "e pluribus unum." As the nation weakens, Democrats grow stronger.

Each party has performed important services in its historical role. Democrats have historically shown greater skepticism about the nation's image of itself as always right, always innocent, always pure. This skepticism is often justified and useful even when mistaken. In moments when Americans are tempted to abuse their power or disregard the legitimate concerns of others, those who issued prophetic warnings have been Democrats more often than not. But when the nation's sovereignty is threatened, when its interests need to be defended, when its values require more than lip service—at those moments, it is usually the Republicans to whom the nation turns.

Peter Beinart, former editor of the liberal *New Republic* magazine, collected some amazing polling data about the modern Democrats in a book he published in 2006. Asked in early 2005 to describe their top foreign-policy priority, self-described conservatives listed "destroying al Qaeda." The top priority of self-described liberals? "Withdrawing from Iraq." As their number-two foreign-policy goal, conservatives listed halting the spread of nuclear weapons to hostile groups or nations. The second-place liberal foreign-policy priority: halting the spread of AIDS. By the end of 2005, only 59 percent of Democrats (as opposed to 94 percent of Republicans) still approved of the Afghanistan war. Only 57 percent of Democrats (as opposed to 95 percent of Republicans) would favor the use of force to destroy a terrorist training camp.[7]

Democrats are not pacifists exactly. But they do recoil from force unless it has some kind of international authorization. And international authorization is not easily obtained. You might be able to persuade international electorates to approve international humanitarian rescue missions like that in Kosovo. But the use of military force to advance specifically American national interests and to assert distinctively American values—that will not easily garner the kind of international backing that Democrats crave.

A Gallup poll conducted *the week after 9/11* found that only 29 percent of the French, 21 percent of Italians, 18 percent of the British, 17 percent of Germans, and 12 percent of Spaniards supported military action against countries that harbored terrorists.[8] In 2004, John Kerry again and again reminded audiences that the French newspaper *Le Monde* had headlined its post-9/11 editorial "We Are All Americans." He did not remind his listeners of the words below the headline: "[T]he reality is perhaps also that of an America whose own cynicism has caught up with [it]."

Voters understood very well the inhibitions and qualms that would have hobbled a Democratic president's response to 9/11. It's hard to win a war when you instinctively flinch from force, hard to summon the nation to unity when it is diversity that delights you, hard to lead a nation you are not sure you love.

Americans trusted Republicans instead—and to our shame, in many important ways, we have let them down. 9/11 changed American politics, but it did not sufficiently change us. At a time when Americans hungered to do something for the nation, the Bush administration could not think of anything for them to do. The administration rearranged the various federal programs to promote volunteering into a new organization grandiloquently called the USA Freedom Corps. The President gave speeches urging Americans to volunteer 4,000 hours of their time to community service. It is hard to say for sure, but there does seem to have been a slight pickup in volunteering after 9/11.[9] The trend did not last, in large part because the things the President asked people to volunteer to do seemed so patently unrelated to the threats the nation faced. Had the President requested a gasoline tax, Congress would gladly have assented—and the debt incurred in the war on terror would not lie so heavy on the Treasury. He did not do so. Had he called for 100,000 volunteers for the military, he might have rallied the nation's youth. Had he urged Arabic-speaking Americans to offer their services to the FBI, CIA, and NSA, he would have enhanced the nation's intelligence agencies and empowered the best elements in Middle Eastern immigrant communities. Those things did not

happen either. At the moment the nation was listening most atten-
tively, we did not call it to meaningful or relevant action.

It is not too late to repair our fault. From foreign policy to health
care, from immigration to energy, this is a moment when a great
national constituency is gathering for change and reform.

Republicans should seize the moment—and champion reform.

Why don't we acknowledge the glaring truth that living standards are stagnating for Americans in the middle, and offer better
answers than the reactionary liberalism of the Democrats?

Why shouldn't we claim universal health insurance as our issue,
while holding fast against state control and government monopoly?

Why cannot the party of national security also deliver border
security?

Why must the party that Americans trust to defend them against
their enemies so often unnecessarily offend and irritate America's
friends?

The American nation has solved many of the problems that
defined the politics of the 1970s and 1980s. Now there are new
challenges—and they call for new creativity.

America's war on terror is not being won; the struggle for world
economic leadership looks to many as if it is being lost.

Standards of living are stagnating for the American middle class
because health care costs zoom uncontrollably.

High energy costs transfer the world's wealth to thug regimes,
even as evidence accumulates of serious environmental risks from
the fuels we burn.

The United States seems increasingly divided by race and class,
and individual Americans express mounting alienation from their
political system.

New medical technologies offer dazzling cures and therapies—
and present horrifying moral dilemmas.

Instead of addressing these challenges, the American political
system seems capable only of polarizing over them. The U.S. gov-

ernment struggles to solve the problems of the twenty-first century with institutions mostly created between 1913 and 1965. From 9/11 to the reconstruction of Iraq to Hurricane Katrina, we have seen crucial institutions fail spectacularly under stress. We pay less attention to how those institutions fail unspectacularly under conditions of nonstress. Bureaucracies that take forever to approve healing drugs; infrastructure neglected and corroding; military hospitals that fail to treat the wounded with dignity; international broadcasting agencies that cannot decide what their mission is: The list of underperformers grows and grows, as the world changes and government fails to change with it.

The future of conservatism as a philosophy—and the Republican Party as an institution—depends on our ability to produce better solutions to these problems and others than we have produced till now. We have long been the party of liberty, and the party of liberty we must remain. The United States may have rejected smaller government. It surely does not need bigger government. But this is not 1964. The ideal under threat today is not the nation's liberty, but the nation's security, its unity, its effectiveness, and—yes, Republicans can care about this, too—its beauty. It was one of the greatest of conservatives, Edmund Burke, who declared that to be loved, a nation must be lovable. A nation that preserves its natural environment, that protects its endangered species, and whose cities delight the eye is a nation more lovable than one that shrugs off despoliation, extinction, and ugliness as the necessary price of freedom.

To vindicate our claim to be the party of the nation, we must make clear that we value public service as much as private wealth creation; that we appreciate the duties of government fully as much as we defend the rights of the marketplace. We cherish our principles, but our first principle is the public good. From Lincoln to Churchill to Reagan, the greatest conservatives have recognized that sometimes the only way to conserve is to change.

FOUR

GOAL ONE:
A Better Deal for the Middle Class

Historians someday will be puzzled to understand: Why were the politics of the 1990s and 2000s so bitter?

Rarely in American history did the substantive policy differences between the two parties shrink so narrowly as in the years from 1995 to 2005. After the loss of Congress in 1994, Bill Clinton swung his party sharply to the right. He endorsed free trade, balanced budgets, and welfare reform. He signed into law a big cut in the capital gains rate and abandoned any talk of major new social programs. Then, after his narrow win in 2000, George W. Bush swung his party equally sharply to the left. He created the first new federal entitlement program since 1974,[1] increased federal education spending by 60 percent, and boosted social welfare and foreign aid spending dramatically.

And yet over those same years, the two parties seethed in rage at each other. Accusations, investigations, and threats of impeachment flew back and forth. America's leading conservative voice, the *Wall Street Journal* editorial page, gave serious credence to allegations that

President Clinton had been implicated in drug smuggling and murder in Arkansas. America's leading glossy magazine, *Vanity Fair,* respectfully profiled two college students who had produced an Internet documentary accusing the U.S. government of destroying the World Trade Center, inviting readers to view the documentary and "decide for themselves."[2]

On their domestic policy records, Bill Clinton and George W. Bush rank as middle-of-the-road presidents, far less radical than, say, Ronald Reagan or Harry Truman. Yet both Truman and Reagan drew support from across the partisan spectrum, while Clinton and Bush polarized the country. On the eve of Bush's second inaugural in 2005, polls showed him with 91 percent approval among Republicans but only 22 percent among Democrats. Clinton faced almost exactly the same approval gap in reverse in January 1997.[3]

But, of course, the question answers itself. It was precisely because the substantive policy differences between the parties were so small that the anger between them raged so hot.

Through most of modern American history, one party or the other has enjoyed a clear political advantage over the other. From 1894 until 1930, Republicans predominated. From the New Deal to Vietnam, Democrats did. The pendulum swung back to the GOP under Nixon and Reagan. But since 1992, political supremacy in the United States has been up for grabs. In three presidential elections in a row—1992, 1996, 2000—the winning candidate failed to win a majority of the popular vote. That had not happened since the aftermath of Reconstruction. For a decade and a half, both parties have sensed realignment lurking just out of reach, and they have struggled and clawed at each other to grasp it.

Why has neither party been able to obtain the advantage?

Part of the answer is that the parties are getting better at their jobs. Try to imagine any contemporary party running a campaign as chaotic, ramshackle, and gratuitously offensive to its core voters as the McGovern campaign of 1972 or the Goldwater campaign of 1964. With polling and focus groups, the parties segment the electorate into ever-smaller slivers and then carefully microtarget each in pursuit of every last possible winnable vote.

But something deeper is going on as well.

Since the late 1970s, the typical middle-of-the-road, middle-class American voter has acquired two huge new worries: the frightening new volatility of the American economy and the disturbing new turbulence in the American family. Voters want answers to both. Instead, they hear Republicans denying that the first concern even exists, and Democrats attacking those anxious about the second as reactionaries and bigots. Democrats stand ready to thrust themselves between Americans and the unruly marketplace. Republicans champion traditional values against a permissive culture. The two parties have entrenched themselves along a great social fault line, seemingly permanently unable to reach across it. Instead, party leaders constantly look over their shoulders, terrified that anything bold or fresh or innovative might provoke some crucial bloc of their followers to defect. It is hard to go forward when you are always looking backward.

Perhaps that is why American politics has so often felt stagnant and cynical over the past two decades.

The booming economy of the Clinton and Bush years delivered large and real prosperity to millions of Americans. By 2005, one out of every six American households enjoyed an income in excess of $100,000 per year. Seven million Americans owned vacation homes, a luxury once so rare that the Census did not even bother to keep tally until 1970. More than 11 million Americans took an ocean cruise in 2005, up from just 500,000 in 1970.[4] Residential cleaning services ranked as the second-fastest-growing industry in America between 1995 and 2005. The United States had created history's first mass upper class.

And tens of millions of Americans who had not quite achieved affluence still enjoyed unprecedented comfort and security. Half of all the married families in the United States earned at least $70,000 in 2003,[5] enough to buy a reasonably pleasant life pretty much anywhere off the island of Manhattan. Half of all American retirees in 2004 had accumulated a net worth of at least $250,000—more than three times as much (adjusting for inflation) as retirees in the middle 1980s.[6]

This was not an economy that reserved its prizes for a favored few super-rich, although of course the super-rich did pretty well. When *Forbes* magazine created its famous 400 list in 1982, it took only $90 million to qualify for the list. By 2006, it took a cool billion.

Millions and millions of American families shared in the good times. Millions and millions more, however, did not. Between 1995 and 2003, the incomes of the poorest one-fifth of Americans actually declined.[7] People who bought even modestly into the stock market or the housing market at the beginning of the boom ended up much richer than their neighbors who went into debt instead. People who got and stayed married fared better than those who lived alone, who split up, or who had their children outside marriage. People with capital assets fared better than those who relied solely on wages. People who employed immigrant labor profited; people who competed against immigrant labor lost.

These trends may explain why the University of Michigan's consumer confidence surveys in the summer of 2006 were detecting the widest gap in a generation between the economic mood of upper-income and lower-income Americans.[8] Altogether, the five years between 2000 and 2006 constitute the longest period since the 1970s in which the earnings of the median American worker stood no higher at the end than they did at the beginning.[9] In this first decade of the twenty-first century, a majority of Americans in this usually optimistic country pessimistically expect that their children will have to endure a lower standard of living than that which the current generation enjoys.[10]

For all the talk of compassion, Republican governance since 2001 has not served the bottom half of American society well. But equally obviously, the Democrats had no plausible alternatives to offer an anxious middle.

Just look at the legislative program of the Democratic Congress elected in 2006. The Pelosi Democrats promised to raise the minimum wage, cut the interest rate on student loans, enhance the negotiating power of trade unions, subsidize favored energy sources, and force pharmaceutical companies to cut their prices.

Who gains from these policies? Not the public as a whole. Not the middle class. Today's Democrats have reverted to the predatory liberalism of the 1970s and 1980s, which sprinkles money upon the influential few at the expense of the unwary many.

Union contracts are often tied to the minimum wage. An increase in the legal minimum bumps up the pay of established workers— while reducing jobs available to the young and unskilled.

Subsidizing interest rates on student loans redistributes income from the population as a whole to college graduates—that is, to the top one-third of the population. The better-off gain; the poorer lose.

Enhancing the negotiating power of trade unions might well raise wages for the tiny unionized portion of the private-sector workforce. The same policy will surely raise prices for the non-unionized 90 percent. The organized gain; the unorganized lose.

As for subsidizing alternative energy, the big question is: Who decides where the subsidies go? If a Democratic Congress ends up writing special favors into law for pet industries, then the politically well-connected gain; energy consumers and taxpayers lose.

Forcing price cuts on pharmaceutical companies would cut into the profits with which those companies finance new investments.

Today's elderly gain lower prices; tomorrow's elderly lose drugs that might have been invented—but now won't be.

The Democratic congressional program transfers wealth from young to old, from poor to rich, from the unorganized to the organized, from the favored to the disfavored, from outsiders to insiders.

Democratic presidential candidate John Edwards presented himself both as the champion of the poor and the candidate of organized labor. But of course you cannot be both. No two interests in American society conflict more radically than the interests of organized labor and the nonorganized poor. Organized labor wishes to restrict access to job markets; the unorganized poor benefit from widened access. Organized labor wishes to exclude cheap foreign products from U.S. markets. The unorganized poor, counting every penny, must buy as cheaply as possible.

Voters sense this truth. It's an observable fact that those voters who care most deeply about equality—deeply enough to organize their lives to live in egalitarian communities—overwhelmingly vote Republican.

Take a look at a map of the state of Missouri. A recent study conducted by the state identified a dozen of the state's 114 counties as "equality centers." These equality centers were located on the outer fringes of St. Louis, Kansas City, Columbia, and Springfield.[11] Every single one of these highly egalitarian areas of the state voted overwhelmingly Republican.

Meanwhile, the most unequal parts of Missouri, the cities and especially the city of St. Louis, voted heavily Democratic. Where you find many different lifestyles and races; where you find singles, immigrants, and gays; where you find high-rise buildings, country estates, and really great take-out—there you find inequality. After all, what is inequality but another form of "diversity"? And what is "equality" but another word for homogeneity? Communities with lots of married families, lots of single-family homes, and low proportions of nonwhite minorities and single people—communities that Democrats and liberals would inwardly disparage as "white bread"—are communities in which people tend to earn similar amounts of money.

A stark demonstration of this point can be seen in Missouri's Third Congressional District, represented for many years by former House Minority Leader Richard Gephardt. Missouri's Third extends both into the city of St. Louis proper and into suburban St. Louis County. The urban part of Gephardt's old district ranks among the very most inegalitarian places in all Missouri: It takes in the gentrifying neighborhoods of University City and the Central West End, where live St. Louis's highly educated, its very rich, its wine drinkers, and its gays. Here Gephardt won 69 percent of the vote in 2002, his last campaign.[12] The suburban portion of Gephardt's district shows far more economic equality. In this part of his district, Gephart won only 55 percent in 2002.

It's important to understand that in highly inegalitarian places, Democrats do at least as well with the rich as they do with the poor. As two Democratic experts concluded after reviewing data from the 1992, 1996, 2000, and 2004 elections: "The Democratic Party has engaged in campaigns that have resonated with the rich and the poor. Meanwhile, it is the Republicans who are winning the hearts and minds of Middle America."[13]

The pattern holds nationwide. Washington, D.C., is the most Democratic city in the country. It is also the most unequal of the nation's forty largest cities,[14] followed closely by New York, Boston, and San Francisco[15]—Democratic strongholds all.

The nation's most equal cities, by contrast, sound like a roll call of the Republican caucus of the Conference of Mayors: Anaheim, Norfolk–Virginia Beach, Indianapolis, Fort Worth, Phoenix, Las Vegas, Charlotte.

The differences between the equal and unequal cities are huge: In Democratic Manhattan, the richest one-fifth of the population earn an average of fifty-two times as much as the poorest one-fifth.[16] In Republican Anaheim, the richest one-fifth earn only ten times as much as the poorest one-fifth.

The trends hold at the state level as well. In 2004, George Bush won seven of the ten most equal states in the country, including Nebraska, Utah, and Indiana. John Kerry won three of the four most unequal, including New York, California, and Louisiana.

The voters in the middle vote Republican. If only for the sake of self-preservation, Republicans should offer them a better deal.

Our better deal should focus on four great anxieties of modern middle-class life: schools, health care, retirement, and the unaccountability of politics and politicians.

A Better Deal for Schools

When Americans think about economic security, they look first to money in the bank—then next to the diplomas on their wall. In 1973, a college-educated thirty-year-old man could expect to earn on average twice as much as a high-school graduate. By 1990, the college graduate was earning three times as much. Americans noticed the change and began worrying: "How will my kids do in this more demanding economy?" By the middle 1980s, education began consistently appearing among the top three issues in national opinion surveys.

As an issue, education has consistently favored Democrats over Republicans. The public has unfortunately accepted the endlessly repeated insistence of teachers' unions and other interest groups that the schools fail because they are starved of resources. Even as education spending has doubled in real terms and then doubled again—even as teacher salaries have risen above those paid to mechanical engineers, psychologists, chemists, architects, and economists[17]—the public has continued to believe that still more money will do the job that all the money paid to date has failed to do.

Despite its many flaws, George Bush's No Child Left Behind law gives conservatives and Republicans an opportunity to open America's eyes and change Americans' minds. Under No Child Left Behind, parents have to confront the actual performance of their own school in comparison to all other schools in their state. The law also provides that schools that do especially badly over a five-year period will be labeled "persistently failing." In spring 2006, Education Secretary Margaret Spellings delivered the first report required by No Child Left Behind. She announced that more than 1,700 U.S. schools had persistently failed to meet state standards for five consecutive years. About 170,000 children in Los Angeles attend persistently failing schools; 125,000 in New York City; and 120,000 in Chicago.

Each and every year to come there will be another report, another head count of children failed. This head count will pose a challenge that will baffle today's Democratic Party. That party has one big educational idea: Spend more on what does not work.

The Democratic Party lives in thrall to the special interests that have wrecked the schools: the teachers' unions and the local political machines controlled by the unions. The unions and the local politicians have built school systems almost perfectly designed to repel the talented and attract the mediocre; to repel the enthusiastic and reward the exhausted. The American educational system pays its highest salaries and most generous benefits to the oldest teachers—even though research strongly suggests that it is the worst teachers who stay longest in the classroom. A high-quality teacher is only about half as likely to make it to the seven-year mark as a low-quality teacher.[18] Meanwhile, eager and talented young people are discouraged by very low starting salaries from trying teaching for a few years in their twenties before moving on to another career. And of course in the poorest districts, where parents are least effective, the worst teachers enjoy the greatest protection.

But while the poorest children suffer most, the low quality of American schooling damages the prospects of the middle class too. Aware that college graduates earn more, middle-class Americans have pushed their children to attend and finish college. Between 1979 and 2004, the proportion of people aged twenty-five to twenty-nine with a bachelor's degree has jumped from one out of every four to one out of every three.[19] All this education does not come cheap. Between 1989 and 2005, tuition costs rose at double the rate of general inflation. This spending is buying a dwindling return. Over the years 2000–2004, the wages of college graduates actually declined by 5 percent.[20]

What's going on? High school seniors who do not know much math and science turn into college graduates who do not know much math or science either. The expensive diploma on the wall may impress the neighbors. But it does not impress the pharmaceutical company deciding whether to locate its new lab in Boston or Bangalore.

As Americans cease measuring educational success by the degrees their children accumulate—and instead by the knowledge and creativity of their children's minds—they will be forced to recognize that the crisis of the inner-city school is the crisis of the leafy suburban school as well. The practice of measurement will create demand for measurable success. That demand can only be met by choice and competition: charter schools, funding that follows the student, and—yes—vouchers where possible and necessary.

Governor Mark Sanford of South Carolina has led a gallant fight for six years to advance competition, proposing tuition tax credits for families earning less than $75,000 and supporting members of the state legislature who proposed voucher programs for special-needs students. His measures fell only just short of being passed. But he increased his majority of the vote in 2006 over 2002, and he consistently ranked among the most popular Republican governors in the country. Instead of deploying education as an issue, Sanford embraced it as a cause. Here is a standard the whole party should, can, and must meet.

A Better Deal for Health Care

Of all the anxieties gnawing at middle-class Americans, it is health care that bites most sharply. Remember I mentioned above that the average worker had not seen a raise in six years under George Bush? Don't blame his stingy employers. Employers during the Bush years paid handsomely for labor. In fact, employers' cost for employing a typical, median worker jumped from $19.85 per hour in 2000 to $25.67 in 2006.[21] That's a raise of more than $5 per hour, or 25 percent.

Yet the average worker saw none of that money. Every dime—and then some—was gobbled up by the rising cost of employer-provided health insurance. Between 2000 and 2006, the typical health-insurance policy for a family of four doubled in cost, from about $6,000 per year to nearly $12,000. Since employers pay about three-quarters of the cost of health insurance, the typical employee cost his or her employer $4,500 more per year in 2006 than the same employee did in 2000. That does not leave a lot of room for wage increases too. That is where your raises went, Mr. and Mrs. America.

You can forgive employees if they do not feel grateful for the extra health care spending. Employees pay about a quarter of the cost of their health coverage directly out of their own pockets. And of course that cost too doubled over the six years from 2000 to 2006.

Look at this from the point of view of some typical American voters. Married, two kids. He's making $45,000 or so per year. Maybe his wife is bringing home another $30,000. They keep about $3,800 in the bank and juggle about $2,200 in credit-card debt.[22] Between 2000 and 2006, their pay has barely gone up at all. They've had a nice little tax cut from the Bush administration, worth perhaps $500 per year to them. But they're paying $1,100 more per year in out-of-pocket health care costs.[23]

These voters are pretty conservative people. They attend church, voted for Bush in 2004, probably in 2000 too. But on health care, their opinions are shifting steadily to the left. Between February 2005 and February 2006, the proportion of Americans who agreed that the health care system needs to be "completely rebuilt" jumped from 21 percent to 32 percent, according to the Pew survey. Another 46 percent wanted to see "major changes" in the health system. Only 20 percent of those surveyed expressed themselves more or less content with the health care status quo.[24]

If conservatives do not take care, this restless public mood could soon create a constituency for a big Canadian-style government health care monopoly. Since 2001, government monopoly care has been endorsed by former Vice President Al Gore,[25] a majority of House Democrats,[26] America's most prominent liberal economist,[27] and both the United Autoworkers and the Service Employees International Union,[28] among many other influential voices. Not all Democrats agree. But many of those who disagree do so for tactical reasons only, preferring to move toward government monopoly by increments rather than by one giant step.

And what will Republicans do? On past experience, we will say "no, no, no" as long as we can, but in the end we will give way—and allow the system to continue its long grinding slide toward ever-greater state control. In President Bush's first term, Medicaid enrolled an additional 1 million participants. His prescription drug bill represents the biggest expansion in the federal role in health care since

1965. And too many of the policy ideas circulating in the Republican world (such as tax credits to help low-wage workers buy private insurance) merely expand the government's responsibility to pay for a failing system—without doing much to fix it.

So what should Republicans do instead? These three things:

Stop Defending the Indefensible

Who agreed that conservatives should defend the dysfunctional American health system from all criticism? Who volunteered to take the bullet for every crummy HMO and overpriced surgeon in the country? Who decided that it was okay with us that tens of millions of Americans would lack health care coverage?

The health care status quo is a nightmare favela of bizarre regulations heaped upon minute controls upon perverse lawsuits upon irrational subsidies. The system has nothing to do with free-market principles. The public hates it. Why should conservatives assume responsibility for protecting it?

Almost everything wrong with American health care can be traced to the malign effects of perverse government policies: perverse tax policy, perverse regulatory policy, perverse spending policy, perverse litigation policy. The U.S. health care system is not a "free-market" system and only barely a "private" system. The federal government is the single largest purchaser of health care in the country, and the federal and state governments combined spend more per American on health care than Canada's federal and provincial governments spend per Canadian: $2,548 in the United States vs. $1,866 in Canada in 2003.[29]

It is state governments, not consumers or insurers, who determine what and who must be insured. If the acupuncture lobby is strong in your state, every policy must cover acupuncture. Ditto marriage counseling. Ditto hairpieces. One industry trade group estimates that the fifty state governments impose a total of some

1,843 must-insure mandates altogether as of mid-2006.[30] The combined impact of these mandates thrusts health insurance costs up to nightmare heights. A health insurance policy for a single twenty-five-year-old man can be bought for less than $1,000 in low-regulation Kentucky. The equivalent policy costs more than $5,800 in high-regulation New Jersey.

So why don't more New Jerseyites complain about these inflated costs? Mostly, because they do not know about them. Very few of them buy their own insurance. Their employers buy it for them. And why is that? Again the answer is: government, government, government. If I buy my own health insurance policy, I have to do it with after-tax dollars. If my employer buys it for me, he can do it with before-tax dollars.

This little fiscal anomaly has come to be as taken for granted by Americans as the designated-hitter rule. Did I say "little"? My mistake: It cost the federal government some $188 billion in forgone revenues in 2005, or about two-thirds of the entire federal deficit. But that's only the beginning of the cost. This anomaly produces much of the frustration and anger that will—if conservatives do not act—sooner or later lead to a government takeover of the whole American health care system.

Present policies prevent health care competition. Maybe some of those overcharged New Jerseyans would like to buy a Kentucky policy? Tough: They cannot.

Present policies discourage the young and healthy from carrying insurance: Insurance just costs too much.

Finally, present policies distort the whole American job market. Workers hesitate to change jobs for fear of losing their coverage. Employers try to control their costs by laying off older workers. The disabled face persistent undeclared discrimination from employers who fear costly health bills.

Why should Republicans champion any of this? Why should we

not be the agents of change? Why not try to think through ways, consistent with our principles, to create incentives for providers to offer better care at lower cost—rather than lose elections making excuses for a government-distorted system that year by year offers worse care at higher cost?

At this late point, it will not be easy to sever the link between employment and insurance. But we can at least begin to try to loosen it.

Massachusetts governor Mitt Romney (aided by experts at the Heritage Foundation) created a private, state-chartered marketplace named "The Connector" that allowed Bay Staters to buy insurance for themselves with untaxed dollars.

President Bush in his 2007 State of the Union address proposed to transform the limitless tax exemption for health insurance into a fixed exemption of up to $15,000 per family.

Republicans in Congress have fought to expand Medical Savings Accounts to help the self-employed buy coverage on the same favorable terms as do people who work for big companies. There are many other solutions as well.

On health care, we conservatives and Republicans should feel our way forward through trial and error. But we should understand our goal: to avert a government takeover of the health care system by fixing the government-created problems that lock millions out of the health care marketplace—in order to deliver affordable health coverage to all.

Define the Unacceptable

If we cannot offer solutions, Democrats and liberals will. They call their solution "single payer." What they really mean is "government monopoly."

Government monopoly offers some up-front advantages. It is cheap—or anyway, it looks cheap. Since government is the only buyer, it gets to set prices. And it usually sets them low: Canada, Britain, and the European health systems spend about 10 percent of gross domestic product rather than the 14 percent and rising of the United States.

Democrats and liberals do not like the word "controls." They hide behind euphemisms like "using [the government's] purchasing power to negotiate lower prices."[31] Negotiations with a single buyer, though, rapidly reduce themselves to the kind of deal making only Tony Soprano could love.

But the real victims of price controls are not the sellers. (Eventually, they hire lobbyists who soften the government's tough line.) The real victims are the system's users. Price controls hold prices down, yes, but always in the least innovative, least responsive, least intelligent way. As conservatives, we do not defend any particular corporation or industry. We hold no brief for pharmaceutical manufacturers or insurance companies. We uphold one principle: open, free competition. Only competition can restrain health price inflation, while maintaining medical quality and delivering medical improvements desired by consumers. And the profit motive is essential to drive competition. Fantasies of "managed competition" or government-directed competition should deceive no one. They are only monopolies by another name.

Government monopolies control costs by forcing people to wait longer for health care. Delay shifts the cost of care from the insurer to the patient, who pays in prolonged absence from work, in pain or anxiety, and—in extreme cases—in heightened risk of death. The United States has the best cancer-survival rates in the advanced world. The most tightly state-controlled health care system in Europe, Britain's, has the worst. In fact, American cancer-survival rates are almost double Britain's.[32]

To save the government money, Canadians wait up to a year for hip replacements and other life-enhancing surgeries.

German doctors earn less than their French or British counter-parts—and only about half as much as American doctors.[33] Thousands of doctors have left Germany for other EU countries, especially Britain. Young Germans shun the medical profession: Fewer than one-fifth of German doctors are under age thirty-five.[34] Germany was hit by waves of doctors' strikes and protests in 2006. France's widely praised health care system faces a deficit projected to triple between 2005 and 2010, and then to double again by 2020.

Across Europe and Canada, governments control the price of prescription drugs to hold medical costs down. In the United States, Congressional Democrats demand that the government do the same.[35] These controls also exact a price: They stifle investment and research. Until very recently, more drug research was done in Europe than in the United States. But as European nations tightened their price controls, the European market became less profitable—and European drug companies concentrated more of their research in the United States. The British drug giant Glaxo moved its main research facility to the United States as early as 1983. Between 1993 and 1997, European researchers produced eighty-one unique new drugs as compared to only forty-eight in the United States. Between 1997 and 2002, the United States outproduced Europe 2 to 1.[36] If present trends continue, more than twice as much will be spent on drug innovation in America as in Europe by 2012.[37]

Americans are anxious about the affordability of health care. It is not much of a favor to them to promise to control costs by denying them new drugs and reduce their odds of beating cancer and other diseases. But that is what is coming, unless conservatives can do better.

Face Reality

Democrats and liberals talk as if the U.S. health care system were a Dickensian nightmare in which the wretched poor expire miserably for lack of care. But poor Americans do get care, often quite lavish care. More than 45 million Americans were covered by Medicaid in 2005. Since 1985, federal law has imposed severe penalties on any hospital that turns away patients for inability to pay. The federal government also funds networks of community health centers to treat the uninsured: Under President Bush, spending on these centers nearly doubled.[38]

If the poor get covered by Medicaid, who are the uninsured? Amazingly often, they are not poor at all. In 2003, almost one-third of the uninsured lived in households with annual incomes above $50,000 and one in five lived in households earning more than $75,000 annually.[39]

Why do these unpoor Americans go uncovered? Probably because they regard health insurance as a bad deal, particularly if they are self-employed or must pay with after-tax dollars. Rather than pay thousands for an overpriced policy, they may decide it makes more sense (especially if they are young and healthy) to take the risk of going without. They can pay ordinary medical bills out of their pocket—and gamble on the emergency room should they get seriously ill.

This gamble often goes wrong. Guess who pays then? You do. The Kaiser Family Foundation estimates that in 2004, hospitals provided some $41 billion worth of care to the uninsured.[40] This cost had to be borne by somebody, and of course it was: Fifty-eight percent of the bill was absorbed by the federal government, another 27 percent by state governments. Most of the remainder was just quietly padded into the bills of the paying customers.

So the great American health care problem is not (or not primarily) figuring out how to get health care. It is a problem of paying for it—specifically, of figuring out how to pay for it in ways that do not bankrupt patients or bleed the Treasury. Perverse incentives, irrational rules, cost-inflating bureaucracies: These are the core of the problem, and these are the failures conservatives should be attacking. Competition works in health care, as it does everywhere else. For all its other faults, the new prescription-drug benefit did institute effective competition among insurance plans. The surprise result: A program expected to cost $38.1 billion in its first year actually cost $30.5 billion, 20 percent under budget.[41]

Conservatives should work for effective competition throughout the health care system. But conservatives must also remember that in a system that has been distorted away from market competition as radically and as long as health care has, the conditions for competition must be created. As in Russia after communism, it won't be enough to declare, "OK, you are all free." Rather than "manage" competition out of existence, governments must nurture competition into being. For starters, states and the federal government will have to prod and force health care providers into publishing their prices and results in ways that allow consumers to make intelligent comparisons. As David Gratzer, himself a doctor, bitingly notes in his brilliant study *The Cure:*

> In 2003, when my wife ruptured a disc in her spine, I set about to find her a neurosurgeon in western New York. Uninsured and uninformed, I resorted to cold-calling neurologists, asking for their opinions of reputable surgeons. Few were willing to speak to a stranger about a colleague's skills. Meanwhile, having a choice of two hospitals and no information on either, we selected one at random and then spent a nervous night before the operation at a Hampton Inn, which I had chosen after reviewing detailed reports at Hotels.com. I found myself musing darkly that for a mundane accommodation decision, we had a surplus of data, whereas for a critical medical decision, we had little or nothing to go on.[42]

Once a system is distorted as badly by government intervention as American health care, you cannot reach a libertarian result simply by standing back and doing nothing. Leaving things alone simply invites more spiraling inflation, more loss of coverage, more human tragedies, more anger and resentment—and then ultimately more government intervention.

In Massachusetts, Governor Romney required all state residents to buy health insurance, with subsidies to those who needed help. The Cato Institute's Michael Tanner denounced the governor's mandate as "an unprecedented level of interference with individual choice and decision-making." Hardly unprecedented: Massachusetts has required automobile drivers to carry insurance since 1927. Governments (rightly) command hospitals to treat all comers. So long as they do, the decision to go uninsured is a decision to shift one's personal costs onto the shoulders of others.

The great nineteenth-century libertarian philosopher Herbert Spencer believed it an outrageous violation of personal liberty to require vaccinations. Few would endorse that view now. If you choose to go unvaccinated, you put not only yourself but everyone else at risk.

As medical costs have increased, as the cost has been spread first through private insurance then through social welfare programs, our choices inevitably become less and less "personal."

What could be more personal than what I eat or drink? And yet when one in five American adults is obese or overweight, eating habits cease to be quite so personal. Obesity rates have been rising steadily as the baby boomers age—with the fastest increases among the fattest Americans, those more than 100 pounds overweight. As things are going, obesity may cause the baby boomers to end up as the first American generation to be less healthy than their parents. The sharp rise in disability claims among the boomers, for example, seems traceable to the rise in boomer obesity.

The Centers for Disease Control estimate that obesity and over-weight added about 10 percent to America's total health costs in the year 2000. If current trends continue, obesity and overweight will add 20 percent to health costs as early as the year 2020.[43]

So my overeating ends up on your tab for health insurance, Medicaid, Medicare, disability pensions, worker's compensation, and other benefits, public and private.

Democrats and liberals will surely try to make use of the obesity issue in the years ahead. They will blame obesity on the sinister machinations of big corporations. They will call for more federal regulation of everything from the fat content of cookies to the length of elementary school recess—and they will do their utmost to green-light a new generation of lawsuits by their trial lawyer campaign donors. As we have seen, those who blame their misfortunes on others tend to vote Democratic, and here is a misfortune for which millions of Americans will want to shift blame.

Republicans will want no part of that. But we have to be careful. Industry groups bearing names like "Consumer Freedom" react furiously against any action aimed at fighting obesity, even steps as seemingly uncontroversial as banning sugared soda from public schools. The freedom to have others underwrite your bad choices is not the kind of freedom Republicans should champion.

One of the 2008 Republican presidential candidates, Arkansas Governor Mike Huckabee, dropped 100 pounds and kept them off with vigorous diet and exercise. Huckabee's story of personal responsibility and triumph is as relevant to our time as Franklin Roosevelt's battle with polio was to his era—and when contrasted to the coming wave of Democratic-favored anti-fat lawsuits, it sends a powerful message about the different characters of the two big parties.

Why shouldn't Republicans adopt the obesity issue as our own? As we work to help individuals take responsibility for their own health coverage, why not speak out against this latest threat to public health, in the way that Richard Nixon signed into law the Surgeon General's warning against cigarette smoke? Not to legislate, but to raise awareness—and to change social expectations and standards.

We are the party that worries most about the rising cost of government. We should not let interest groups or exaggerated ideology detour us away from that core commitment, in health care or anywhere else.

Medicaid in particular will have to be handed over in full to the states. Right now, the federal government picks up a large portion of state Medicaid costs—tempting states to enrich and expand their Medicaid programs in full knowledge that they will have to pay one-half or less of the cost. Cost sharing invites irresponsible spending. Between 1980 and 2005, the total cost of the Medicaid program quintupled—and that's adjusting for inflation.[44]

The next Republican president should alert the states: What you got last year is the same amount you will get next year and the year after. Within those limits, you are free to run your program any way you like. The federal government will end its role as the overseer and master of state health programs. The Democrats may suspect that state governments yearn to condemn their people to neglected squalor; Republicans trust the people in the states to govern themselves at least as wisely as those same people do through their representatives in Washington.

The U.S. health industry is colossal, with thousands of moving parts and dozens of powerful constituencies. Instead of inventing some grand master plan, the next Republican president should see himself as the modern equivalent of the trustbusters of the early twentieth century. His job is to identify obstacles to competition, one by one—and break them. Most of these obstacles have been created by government, often by state governments. The next Republican president cannot bark orders at the states. But he can use his power over Medicaid funding to push states toward competition, individual ownership, and cost control. At a minimum, he can propose legislation to allow customers to buy interstate health insurance—so New Jerseyites can buy themselves some of that low-cost Kentucky coverage.

The barriers to effective concentration are huge and fiercely defended: It will be the work of a generation to cast them down. Waging this fight will be an opportunity as well as a challenge: an opportunity for Republicans to overcome the conservatism of the status quo and rediscover their instincts as Reaganite and Thatcherite radicals for change.

A Better Deal for Retirement

Social Security is shaping up to be one of the greatest rip-offs in the history of government finance. Social Security is advertised as a government-guaranteed savings plan. You pay your money in; you get an annuity out. Campaigning for a Social Security plan in the 1930s, Franklin Roosevelt would wave a mock-up of an individual passbook as a prop. To this day, Social Security mails out individual statements, detailing how much you have contributed in payroll taxes and how much pension you can expect to receive in return.

If you were born before 1950, the deal will look quite attractive. Assuming a normal lifespan, you should collect many hundreds of thousands of dollars more in benefits than you paid in contributions. But if you were born after 1970, you can expect to earn only a little better than a 1 percent return on your money. And if you were born after 1980, you would do better to stuff your Social Security contributions into your mattress.

Social Security represents an increasingly bad deal for younger workers. And because it is such a costly bad deal, it precludes many workers from saving for themselves.

A worker earning $40,000 per year pays almost $5,000 a year into

Social Security (half of that money is remitted directly by his employer, but it still ultimately comes out of the worker's compensation). Over a working lifetime, that's more than $200,000 in contributions—or ten times as much as the typical family is able to save in its IRAs, 401(k)s, and bank accounts.[45]

Invested in a mutual fund earning the historic average return on equities, about 8 percent, that $200,000 would increase in value to $2,000,000 over the worker's lifetime. Contributed to Social Security, $200,000 will buy a pension worth a little more than $16,000 per year.

Even a worker who never earns more than the minimum wage could retire with almost $600,000 in assets after forty-five years of labor, assuming an 8 percent annual return. A worker who never earns more than $10 an hour could retire with just shy of a million.

By contrast, President Bush's tentative Social Security plan never did inspire anyone. Some misguided pollster or focus group discouraged the President from talking about personal ownership and wealth. Instead the President tried to frighten workers into accepting his plan with warnings of the impending insolvency of Social Security. His plan horribly backfired: The more he scared Americans, the more they clung to the old and familiar.

In the end, ironically, it was Bush who got stampeded by the fears he tried to use. By the end of his campaign, he had virtually dropped all mention of personal accounts to focus instead on proposals to cut Social Security benefits for higher-income retirees. Not a bad idea, but not exactly a big one.

Here's a big one: Revive the plan for personal accounts by reviving a discarded idea from the Clinton administration. (After all, the Democrats are not using it anymore.) In 1997, President Clinton proposed the creation of a personal savings accounts retirement system alongside Social Security. These "USA accounts" would match the savings of lower-income savers dollar for dollar, up to a maximum of $300 per year. Clinton's plan was excessively and unnecessarily complicated. Why create a second government saving scheme to compensate for the failings of the first? That extra $300 per year of government help for low-income workers could achieve some amazing results *within* Social Security. With an extra $300 per year deposited into a personal Social Security account, a minimum-wage worker would retire after forty-five years with almost $700,000 in assets; a $10-an-hour worker would find himself or herself well north of $1.1 million.

That should be our conservative and Republican promise to American workers: "Every American a millionaire by age sixty-seven!"

Some Republicans will look back on the Bush experience and dismiss personal retirement accounts as a losing idea. But this is to ignore how political progress is achieved: step by step.

> Many who before regarded legislation on the subject as chimerical, will now fancy that it is only dangerous, or perhaps not more than difficult. And so in time it will come to be looked on as among the things possible, then among the things probable;—and so at last it will be ranged in the list of those few measures which the country requires as being absolutely needed. That is the way in which public opinion is made.[46]

If change is to come to American politics, however, Republicans and conservatives must first bring change to the American political system—a system that seems to be compacting itself into something that looks uncomfortably like a self-perpetuating, self-protecting oligarchy.

A Better Deal for Democracy

Skillful gerrymandering has entrenched congressional incumbents: With every passing decade, turnover in Congress declines. In the nineteenth century, an incumbent party could drop 125 House seats in a big election like 1894. In a big mid-twentieth-century election like 1930 or 1958, an incumbent party could lose as many as 50. But since the advent of the "campaign reform" era in the mid-1970s, an incumbent party has lost more than 30 House seats only once, in 1994. Single-digit seat shifts have become the norm.

If three decades of misnamed reforms have entrenched incumbents, they have advantaged the wealthy even more. The McCain-Feingold reforms tried to shut down "political action committees" that raised "soft money" from corporations and wealthy donors. McCain-Feingold replaced them with new super–political action committees that act as the personal campaign treasuries of the super-wealthy: the so-called 527s used to such effect by megamillionaires like George Soros and Peter Lewis in the 2004 election cycle.

The super-wealthy enjoy even larger advantages when they seek political office. American voters have appreciated wealthy candidates at least since George Washington poured gallons of drinks for the electors of Alexandria County in 1758. But something new is happening today. The multiplication of gigantic personal fortunes at the top of society—combined with severe restraints on donations by the nongigantically rich—have together acted to favor candidates who can write checks to their own campaigns.

In 2005, four U.S. senators possessed fortunes of $100 million or more. All of them were Democrats, interestingly: John Kerry, Herb Kohl, Jay Rockefeller, and Jon Corzine. Another twelve Senators possessed fortunes of at least $10 million. The House was not much less plutocratic: At least thirty members of the House were worth $5 million or more.

Of three big races of 2005, two were won by hugely wealthy, self-financed candidates: Jon Corzine in the New Jersey governor's race and Michael Bloomberg in the New York mayoralty. Two of the most dramatic races of 2006 likewise featured self-financed candidates: Ned Lamont, heir to a JP Morgan fortune, challenged Joe Lieberman in the Connecticut Democratic primary; Jim Pedersen, a shopping-mall developer, challenged Republican Jon Kyl in Arizona, in the most expensive race in the state's history. Who would ever think of Mike Bloomberg as a candidate for national office in 2008 but for his bankroll? And how much of the excitement over an Al Gore candidacy in 2008 derived from the widespread hope among Democrats that he could finance much of his own campaign with his Google stock options?

Among nonwealthy candidates, family ties play an ever-larger part in political careers. In 2000, the son of a president and the son of a senator battled for the presidency; of the frontrunners for 2008, one is the wife of a president, another the son of a senator, another the son of a governor. There has been a Bush, Dole, or a Clinton on the ballot in every presidential election since 1972—often two at the same time. Eleven of the 100 senators of the 109th Congress owed their rise to the prior success of an immediate relative: Bayh, Chafee, Clinton, Dodd, Dole, Gregg, Kennedy, Landrieu, Pryor, Rockefeller, and Sununu. The House of Representatives is presided over by the daughter of a former congressman. The whole scene can sometimes remind one of the last days of the Roman Republic, a battleground for family dynasts and their retainers, in which inherited friendships and enmities often matter more than any acknowledged motive.

All political systems generate elites. Democracies, however, legitimately expect their elites to remember that the people chose them—and that it is to the people they owe their accounting. Republicans once looked to term limits to impose that accounting. Unfortunately, the Supreme Court ruled in 1995 that states lacked the power to limit the terms of their representatives in Congress. Probably only a constitutional amendment would do the job. If so, that is a fight worth taking up. We might at the same time adopt the suggestion of those (very non-conservative) law professors who advocate an amendment imposing an eighteen-year term limit for future justices of the Supreme Court, with vacancies staggered to open at regular two-year intervals.

It is perhaps even more important to limit the terms of the chairmen of congressional committees. Republicans voluntarily imposed such limits on themselves during their majority. House Democrats followed in 2007—but their commitment may corrode if their hold on the majority lasts. Why should such limits, so essential to the public welfare, be left to the grace and favor of power holders? Republicans should push to write them into the procedures of Congress, if not federal law.

McCain-Feingold doubles contribution limits for candidates who face self-financed rivals. Why not lift limits entirely for a candidate in such races? Campaign finance restraints above all limit a candidate's time. A Ross Perot or a Michael Bloomberg who can write a $100 million check to his own campaign can devote himself full-time to talking to voters; a competitor who raises his money in $2,300 increments must divert precious days from vote-seeking to raise his $100 million donor by donor by donor. Doubling that limit to $4,600 scarcely helps. Let's even the playing field entirely, not just a little.

Our party, the party of the great American middle, should be the party that reminds America's increasingly self-perpetuating political elites for whom they work and whose values and interests they must honor.

FIVE

GOAL TWO:
Keep China Number Two

Had Germany or Russia emerged as the great dominant power in the struggles of the century just past, what would our planet look like now? If China or India were to emerge as the great dominant power of the century to come, what would our planet look like then?

Every coffeehouse radical can recite the list of America's sins and failings, some of them genuine. But it was an American president, Woodrow Wilson, who promised to make the world safe for democracy. He did not say "American democracy." He said "democracy"—everybody's democracy. Despite inevitable misjudgments, mistakes, momentary weaknesses, and the inevitable trade-offs any global power would face, the United States has striven mightily to honor Wilson's pledge.

Another American president, and another Democrat, Harry Truman, used to carry in his wallet a scrap of paper on which he had copied in his own handwriting some lines from a poem by Alfred Lord Tennyson.

For I dipt into the future, far as human eye could see,
Saw the Vision of the world, and all the wonder that would be. . . .

Till the war-drum throbb'd no longer, and the battle-flags were furl'd
In the Parliament of man, the Federation of the world.

There the common sense of most shall hold a fretful realm in awe,
And the kindly earth shall slumber, lapped in universal law.

Does it seem strange that these should be the favorite verses of the man who dropped the atomic bomb on Hiroshima and Nagasaki? Who created the Central Intelligence Agency and fought the Korean War? It should not. All our hopes for universal law—the aspirations dream of liberalism at its best—all our dreams of a better world—and even all our vision for a world that someday overcomes the narrow limits of nationalism—rest upon the hard fact of American national power. That power, in turn, rests on American economic supremacy, a supremacy now challenged by the renaissance of Asia.

At home, Americans' hopes for fairness and justice—for enhanced security and a better deal—likewise depend on the nation's economic success. And that prosperity and success is today threatened as it has not been threatened in decades by a resurgence of a dangerous pseudo-populism that exploits the unease of lower-income Americans to advance a special-interest agenda that will wreck the prosperity that supports all our hopes.

For some Democrats and liberals, the pessimistic national mood of the 2000s represents a golden opportunity to revert to the disastrous and discredited Big Government interventionism of the past.

Three of the Democratic senators elected in 2006—Ohio's Sherrod Brown, Pennsylvania's Bob Casey Jr., and Virginia's Jim Webb—campaigned as unabashed protectionists. The newest members of the House of Representatives elected in 2006 spoke of finding ways to limit the freedom of companies to fire workers and move factories.[1] Other Democrats have sought to use government muscle to cancel valid oil leases that later proved unfavorable to the federal government—contracts, it might be worth noting, negotiated and signed by the Clinton administration. In 2007, House Democrats passed a bill banning secret ballots in union certification elections.

In 2005, Democrats pushed through the Maryland legislature a law that aimed to force Wal-Mart to spend more on health care. After the law was struck down by federal courts, the unchastened Maryland Democrats announced they would redraft the law and try again. Democrats in San Francisco have voted to impose a health care tax on all local employers, despite warnings that their ordinance also violates federal law. Democratic local governments have imposed super-minimum-wage laws (proponents call them "living wage" laws) in 140 jurisdictions, including not only liberal havens like New York City and San Francisco, but also Sacramento, California; Lincoln, Nebraska; Bloomington, Indiana; and Miami, Florida. In November 2006, Democratic activists persuaded the electorates of six states to raise their local minimum wages by as much as $1.70 over the prevailing federal minimum.

Against this resurgence of the brain-dead statism of the past, the Republican Party must stand as the great guardian of American economic strength and national power against all comers. The party of the nation must also champion national economic power.

In a world of intensifying economic competition, the self-destructive follies proposed by the new pseudopopulist wing of the Democratic Party threaten not just American prosperity, but America's standing in the world.

According to World Bank estimates, in 2005 the U.S. economy outweighed China's by a margin of 5.5 to 1. Suppose for the sake of argument that China's economy were to continue to grow at the 9 percent rate reported in the first years of the century. Under such circumstances, China's economy would grow by 2025 to almost exactly the same size as America's economy had attained in 2005.

If the U.S. economy grew over those same two decades at a 3 percent pace, then the United States would still hold a 2-to-1 economic advantage over China in 2025. But if the U.S. growth rate were to slip to 2 percent—as it did in the 1970s and early 1980s—then the U.S. advantage over China would narrow to barely 3 to 2 by 2025. And if the U.S. economy were to slow to the 1 percent growth rate to which some U.S. allies sank in the 1990s—then by 2025 China would for all practical purposes have caught up.

In times past, Republicans have offered a clear and simple answer to questions about America's future economic growth: cut taxes and reduce regulation.

Those answers have become increasingly inadequate.

We will not soon again be able to offer America a big, broad, middle-class tax cut. The first of the baby boomers will begin to qualify for Medicare and Social Security in 2008. The good news is that baby boomer retirees can reasonably expect another twenty-five years or so of active life. The bad news is that every one of them has been promised twenty-five years' worth of pensions and free health care from the federal government—and that government has absolutely no idea where the money is to come from. Americans have already bought themselves a bigger government. Perhaps some of the purchase can be returned to the store by scaling back some of the baby boomers' benefits. But the boomers are voters, and they are likely to react badly to proposals to trim their benefits. So the great question before the country will be: How on earth do Americans pay for the promises they have already made?

Between 2000 and 2030, the number of Americans older than sixty-five is expected to double, from 35 million to 71.5 million. The number of working Americans is not expected to rise nearly so fast. Today, three workers pay taxes to support each retiree. By 2030, the ratio will have dropped to only two workers per retiree.

That suggests that federal revenues will rise over the next

quarter century much more slowly than the government's spending commitments. The economist Laurence Kotlikoff calculates the gap between the present values of the country's future income and its future spending promises as $65.9 trillion. Lest that figure bounce off the head like some absurd Dr. Evil invention ("one million bajillion dollars"), Kotlikoff offers some comparisons to make sense of it.

To meet a fiscal gap of $65.9 trillion, Kotlikoff estimates, would require either

- an immediate and permanent *doubling of all personal and corporate income taxes*; or

- an immediate and permanent *two-thirds cut in Social Security and Medicare benefits*; or

- an immediate and permanent *cut in federal discretionary spending of 143 percent*—that is, reducing the budgets for defense, homeland security, highway, education, and everything else Congress appropriates to zero—and then finding 43 percent more cuts on top of that.[2]

In the face of such a huge fiscal gap, the days of broad, across-the-board, middle-class tax cutting are over.

The end of the tax-cutting era leaves us with a great problem, however. While conservatives and Republicans have succeeded in reducing the burden of taxation on middle-class incomes, we have not been nearly so successful at cutting taxes on investment and wealth creation. America taxes corporate income at rates up to 39.5 percent. The average corporate tax rate across the twenty-five countries of the European Union is 26.6 percent. America's long-term capital gains tax rate of 15 percent exceeds those of Germany and most Eastern European countries. If current law is not renewed and the capital gains tax rate reverts to 20 percent, America's rate will exceed that of slow-growth France. The estate tax, now scheduled to slide to zero, returns in its full ferocity after 2011.

Republicans and conservatives cannot lead the country to this level of wealth by endlessly reprising (or attempting to reprise) our Greatest Hits of the Reagan Era. We need a new agenda for economic growth and national power: a smarter tax code, fairer laws, and a more skilled population.

Smarter Taxes

Just as spending is preprogrammed to rise over the coming years, so too is the tax burden. The Bush tax cuts are scheduled to expire with the Bush presidency. The ravenous alternative minimum tax (AMT) is poised to gobble up ever more middle-class income. Invented in 1969 to foil tax avoidance by the superrich, the AMT, if unaltered, is projected to touch 30 million taxpayers by 2010 and to collect at least $611 billion in extra revenue over the years from 2006 to 2015.[3]

These preprogrammed taxes will enrich the government. But they will do great damage to the American nation.

The expiration of the Bush tax cuts will raise taxes on work and investment—and the United States urgently needs more of both. President Bush's 2005 commission on tax reform, for example, estimated that cutting taxes on capital investment would add up to 27.9 percent to U.S. capital stock over the ensuing decade and up to 6.0 percent to national income.[4]

Meanwhile, the stealthy rise in the AMT will discourage the formation of human capital. The AMT bears most heavily on upper-middle-income families with children—and the United States urgently needs to encourage its most economically productive citizens to have more children if it is to avoid the decline faced by Europe and Japan.

To accelerate America's rate of growth, we should adopt as our Republican goals a capital gains tax rate of zero, an inheritance tax of zero, a dividend tax rate of zero, and a maximum corporate tax rate of zero.

To defeat the antinatalist effect of the AMT, we should propose to revise the law so that it does not override personal exemptions and the per-child tax credit. Then we should propose to index it permanently to inflation, so that rising price levels do not push middle-class people into a system designed to catch the tax-avoiding rich.

Obviously, this is not a populist tax agenda. To balance it, we enhance fairness by widening health coverage, extending personal ownership of retirement accounts, and improving school quality. Our tax program has a different purpose: to generate the growth and revenue to sustain the nation's wealth—and incidentally pay for its populist benefits.

Again obviously, this is not an inexpensive agenda. The revenue we are cutting will have to be replaced: In the face of multitrillion-dollar deficits, we can no longer cut taxes now and balance the books by promising to cut spending later, maybe.

If we are proposing major tax cuts, we will have to balance them with other tax increases. This idea will, I know, jolt the conservative mind. Since 1982, conservatives have fought hard to prevent the federal government from imposing "new taxes" on the American people. The problem is that our slogan, "Read My Lips: No New Taxes," has translated into practical politics as "Read My Lips: No New Thinking." The ugly fact is that in the absence of new taxes, the United States will have to shoulder steady, stealthy increases in its old taxes—and those old taxes will likely prove vastly more damaging than wisely chosen new taxes need be.

But what kind of new taxes?

The economist Bruce Bartlett argues that a value-added tax

(VAT) offers the best way out for the United States[5]: A VAT taxes consumption, not work or investment, and so can raise large amounts of revenue without unduly slowing economic growth. Former Treasury Secretary Lawrence Summers has joked that the United States remains one of the few advanced countries without a VAT for the reason that "Republicans oppose a VAT because it is a mighty revenue-raising machine, and Democrats oppose it because it is regressive." The punch line: "And the United States will get a VAT when Democrats figure out that it is a mighty revenue-raising machine, and Republicans figure out that it is regressive."

In seriousness, though, no Republican politician would ever advocate a value-added tax. Whatever its economic merits, it is too visible, too burdensome, too novel ever to muster any support in the party. It would expose Republicans to accusations of shifting the tax burden from rich to poor. Political professionals will remember that advocacy of a VAT cost former Democratic Ways & Means Committee Chairman Al Ullman reelection to his House seat in 1980—and that the imposition of such a tax contributed to the destruction of the Canadian Progressive Conservative Party in the election of 1993.

Some conservatives have flirted with the idea of a national retail sales tax as a possible substitute for other federal taxes. Representative Billy Tauzin of Louisiana campaigned for the concept in the 1990s. The libertarian radio host Neal Boortz resuscitated the idea a decade later. Aside from the small problem that the math behind the idea has never quite worked, the national retail tax falls victim to some obvious conceptual difficulties:

- What is "retail"? Will the tax, for example, apply to purchases at Costco and Sam's Club, which advertise themselves as wholesalers?

- Are services exempt? And where do we draw the line between a service and a good? Is a meal in a restaurant a good or a service?

- How do we prevent cheating? Won't we need some kind of enforcement? If so, there go the claims to have repealed the Internal Revenue Service.

- How do we protect consumers from paying a tax upon a tax upon a tax? Imagine a small businessman who must buy a computer (taxed at 17 percent) to serve his customers (also taxed at 17 percent)? Will these taxes compound? Or will we allow him to somehow deduct the taxes he paid from the taxes he charged? In which case, we've just reinvented the VAT—with all its attendant political difficulties.

Instead of a VAT or retail sales taxes, the next Republican president should consider alternative new taxes on consumption as full or partial replacements for the job-killing, wealth-killing, child-unfriendly taxes preprogrammed to take effect after 2010.

The carbon tax I will propose in Chapter 8 is a consumption tax. In fact, the single most amazing thing about this tax—from a political point of view—is that it is one of the few, maybe the only, consumption taxes liberals have ever approved. Consumption taxes have long been condemned as unfair to the poor. The poor consume more of their income than the rich do, so if we tax consumption, we end up taxing the poor on a larger portion of their incomes.

But it does not have to be that way, as an economist named David Bradford brilliantly theorized two decades ago.[6] Bradford began by observing that every dollar an individual receives must either be saved or consumed. That's true by definition: You either use something or you don't—if you don't, you've saved it.

Upon this simple—obvious, really—foundation, Bradford elaborated a powerful new idea.

Suppose the government were to alter individual retirement accounts to let each and every American save as much as they wanted per year—and to withdraw the money whenever he or she wanted.

Those two simple rule changes would together transform the present income-tax system into a consumption-tax system.

Unlike gas taxes and VAT, this new consumption-tax system could charge the richest taxpayers much more than the poorest. That is because the Bradford tax system makes use of existing income-tax mechanisms, and so it can charge a rising rate of tax on rising amounts of spending.

The first, say, $15,000 of spending—the money a family needs to spend to cover its most basic needs—could go entirely untaxed. Rates could rise from there as high as the tax authorities wanted to raise them.

Under Bradford's system, an ordinary American family would notice hardly any changes to their economic life at all. They would file tax returns just as they do now—only, instead of many individual deductions for federally approved expenditures, they would gain one big deduction for all their savings. On everything not saved, they would pay a progressive tax, just as they do now.

It's upper-income taxpayers who would encounter stark new changes. So long as they kept their money saved or invested, they would pay no tax at all. All of today's uncountable tax shelters would be simplified to one big shelter: 0 percent tax on everything you don't spend. And all of today's devices to extract money from the well-to-do would likewise be simplified to: one great big rising rate of tax on everything the well-to-do opt to spend.

The stark new incentives presented to the wealthy by the Bradford tax would ramify through the whole economy. In the first decade of the twenty-first century, American households saved less than 2 percent of their incomes, the lowest personal saving rate ever recorded, and far lower than personal saving rates in almost all other advanced industrial economies. Upper income Americans have reduced their savings and increased their consumption the most: One study conducted for the Federal Reserve Bank of San Francisco found that the top 20 percent of American households had swung from saving 6 percent of their earnings in the early 1990s to spending almost 6 percent more than they earned by the year 2000.[7]

These decisions may not have been irrational: In the 1990s, the top 20 percent saw the values of their houses and stock-market portfolios boom. It was perhaps natural that they would wish to tap into that apparent extra wealth even before they sold their stocks or houses. Then came the proliferation of home equity loans to help them out. But if rational, the American disinclination to save threatens heavy long-term consequences, as the United States prepares both for the coming competition with China and the great retirement of the baby boomers. It threatens some nasty short-term consequences, too: The great housing boom of the early '00s stalled in 2006. If prices were to fall, many once-affluent Americans could abruptly see the equity in their homes disappear. Shifting taxation away from savings and toward consumption could encourage less risky behavior—and greater national wealth over the long term.

From the particular point of view of the well-to-do, even quite heavy taxes on consumption should seem less horrible than the looming alternative: a tax on wealth in the form of inflation. Like people, governments do not do what they cannot do. If they cannot pay their obligations, they do not pay them. For a government, inflation offers a secret and seductive escape from unpayable debt, like the unpayable debt the United States owes in the form of unreformed, unfinanced entitlement programs. You are owed a pension? Fine: The government will print one up for you. The IOU is marked "paid in full," but the payment has been financed by a stealthy tax on the money held by the people. Everybody's money buys just a little bit (or not such a little bit) less. The more money you have, the worse inflation hurts you. If the United States does not solve its entitlements problem now, get ready for a bad burst of inflation sometime around 2030. With taxes as with everything else in life, the rule is: Pay me now or pay me more later.

Fairer Laws

In the 1970s and 1980s, Americans freed their economy from the dead hand of government control. We Republicans can take much of the credit, but not all. It was Senator Edward Kennedy who led the deregulation of the airlines. President Carter accepted the need to deregulate the price of natural gas. President Clinton disregarded those who wanted to impose telecommunications regulations on the Internet.

But now the country is in danger of reverting toward the worst habits of the past. Some Democrats want to abolish secret ballots in union certification elections—too inconvenient for their union allies. Others are backsliding toward trade protectionism. Still others wage legislative warfare against Wal-Mart and other companies that bring better choice and service to the poor. Nor is the fault all on one side. George W. Bush imposed tariffs on imported steel. He signed into law the costliest farm bill in history, undoing at a pen stroke the free-market farm reforms of the 1990s. He was stampeded into accepting the mischievous Sarbanes-Oxley bill, a wild over-reaction to the accounting scandals exposed in 2001 and 2002. Americans will be paying for the President's weakness for years to come. Sarbanes-Oxley has helped drive many U.S. companies off public markets into private equity—and has caused many others to consider listing on the less legally hazardous London or Toronto exchanges.

It often seems that while India and China steadily improve their business climates, Americans have decided they can afford to go backward.

They cannot afford it, and it is our job as Republicans and

conservatives to remind them of that fact. We have to fight for open labor markets, for free trade, against abusive lawsuits, against subsidies, for faster approval of patents, for rational treatment of corporations.

We do this to make America great, but we do it also to make America fair. What happens when special interests are allowed to manipulate free markets in their favor? Look at America's trade policy.

Most of us imagine we live in an era of borderless markets. Yet tariffs of from 8 percent to 30 percent are common on low-tech consumer goods like glassware, sneakers, plates, and bicycles. The average rate of tariff on low-tech consumer goods exceeds 10 percent. A single-parent family earning $25,000 per year (the median income for single-parent households) has been estimated to pay as much as an extra $400 per year because of tariff protections.[8]

Federal farm subsidies drive up the price of basic foodstuffs, again a hardship for America's poorest. American consumers pay more than double the world price for sugar, 23 percent more for milk, and 37 percent more for cheese.[9] Subsidies encourage American farmers to grow more bulk commodities—wheat, corn, soybeans, cotton—than Americans can consume. The United States then dumps these subsidized crops on world markets, to the injury of farmers in poorer countries. The British aid organization Oxfam points out that in 2002 the United States paid $3.4 billion in subsidies to cotton growers, double the aid the federal government gave to all of sub-Saharan Africa. In a world market undistorted by subsidy, Africa would emerge as a leading cotton-producing region.[10]

Litigation abuse has transformed the American judicial system into a lottery where most find only delay and frustration, but a lucky few win amazing prizes. George Priest of Yale Law School likes to tell the story of the plaintiff who was exposed to asbestos for one day when his church was renovated, and won a $4.5 million settlement.

The American tort system that yielded this windfall for one happy winner costs the average family more than $800 per year.

Americans were rightly outraged by the failed federal response to Hurricane Katrina. Yet how many understand that it was failed federal policies that exposed New Orleans to such terrible risk in the first place? Reviewing the debacle afterward, the reporters closest to the story agreed that the worst damage was inflicted not by those government agencies that had failed, but by those government agencies that had performed exactly as they were supposed to do.

> The [Army] Corps [of Engineers] spent more in Louisiana than in any other state, but it wasted most of the money on ecologically harmful and fiscally wasteful pork that kept its employees busy and its political patrons happy, while neglecting hurricane protection for New Orleans. One of its pork projects, the Mississippi River Gulf Outlet, actually intensified Katrina's surge. . . . And while it is legitimate to blame Bush for the problems at FEMA and DHS, most of his administration's proposed budget cuts for the Corps were uncharacteristically responsible efforts to block wasteful spending—which is why Congress routinely ignored them.[11]

Yet the same federal government that could not responsibly spend flood-protection money now aspires to play venture capitalist in the automobile industry. The Clinton administration spent $1.8 billion developing an alternative to the internal combustion engine. The Bush administration has requested $1.2 billion to the same purpose—disregarding a generation of evidence that governments make lousy investors.

In the 1970s and 1980s, we conservatives used to burn with indignation at abuses like this. Today, apathy seems to have settled upon us. We seem to have decided we have taken reform about as far as it can go. Yes, President Bush often talked reform. But his administration brought little energy or enthusiasm to the task. It is time to get mad again about the perversities and inefficiencies inflicted by heavy-handed government—and to take up again the cause of those victimized and exploited by government-mandated waste.

A More Skilled Population

The first resources of any society are the skills and capabilities of that society's people. And through most of the twentieth century, the United States could boast a more skilled and capable population than any other major power.

That claim has ceased to be valid. The best data we have strongly suggest that American high-school students lag well behind the norm for other advanced industrial countries in mathematics and slightly behind the norm in science. (U.S. students read about as well as the advanced industrial world average.) This is not, obviously, because Americans are dumber than other people. In fact, American eight-year-olds fall smack in the middle of the industrial world pack. It takes seven years of costly schooling to knock them down to last place.[12]

The U.S. Department of Education candidly acknowledges that American teaching—and especially American teaching of math and science—lags in quality. In 1995, the department commissioned outside experts to videotape eighth-grade math classes in the United States, Germany, and Japan. The experts then rated the quality of the lessons taught in those classes. In Japan, 39 percent of lessons taught received the highest rating. In Germany, 28 percent received the top mark. In the United States . . . zero.[13]

It's important to understand, though, precisely which American children are being failed most badly by this miseducation. One of the most revealing international tests divides students into four categories of mathematical skill. In the United States as elsewhere in the advanced world, most students are pretty ordinary: 64 percent of American and non-American students fall into the two intermediate categories. The big difference between America and elsewhere is found at the bottom and at the top. While 18 percent of students elsewhere in the developed world achieve the highest level of mathematical proficiency, only 12 percent of American students do. And while 17 percent of students elsewhere in the developed world fell into the lowest category, 24 percent of American students did so.[14]

These are very frightening numbers.

And they get more frightening still.

White and Asian American students score at least as well in every category as their counterparts elsewhere in the advanced industrial world. It is black and Hispanic students who disproportionately fail to reach that top category of highest achievement.

Scores on the Scholastic Aptitude Test give us an exact count of how many minority achievers America is missing. In 2006, 95,000 high-school seniors scored 700 or above on the verbal SAT. Only 1,117 of those students were black. That year, almost 69,000 scored 700 or above on the math SAT. Only 976 of them were black.[15]

Here's one indisputable fact about minority teenagers: They are teenagers. Give them an opportunity to slack off, to take the easy way, to spend time with their friends or their video games rather than to work, and as every parent knows, they will grab it.

There's one great restraint on the natural laziness of the brighter teens—the ambition to be accepted at a good university. But what would happen if you told those kids, "Don't worry, you'll be accepted anyway"? That is exactly the incentive America's affirmative action programs extend to minority (and especially African-American) students, and they respond pretty much exactly as one might expect.

Among the students who took the SAT in 2006:

- 47 percent of white test-takers had studied trigonometry, as opposed to 36 percent of black test-takers.

- 30 percent of white test-takers had studied calculus, as opposed to 15 percent of black test-takers.

- 33 percent of white test-takers had taken honors courses in mathematics, as opposed to 20 percent of black test-takers.

- 41 percent of white test-takers had taken honors courses in English, as compared to 29 percent of black test-takers.[16]

Americans' determination to extend more opportunity to a wronged minority has created incentives that have perversely limited minority opportunities. And as the minority population of the United States grows, the perverse effects of affirmative action are metastasizing into a threat to the educational standards of the whole country.

When affirmative action programs were first introduced into American education in the early 1970s, the targeted population numbered less than 15 percent of all students. It was not wholly unreasonable for decision makers to accept preferential programs as a tolerably costly transition measure from the injustice of segregation to a better, fairer future.

What nobody foresaw back in 1970 was that the population of the most disadvantaged students was about to explode. Between 1970 and 2005, some 40 million people would legally and illegally migrate to the United States. Of these 40 million people, one-third lacked even a high school degree. The children of these new migrants are encountering much more difficulty climbing the ladder of success than the immigrants of the past.

Three-quarters of all migrants to the United States originate in Mexico and Central America. Half of these migrants enter the United States illegally.

Mexicans and Central Americans show the lowest levels of educational attainment of any immigrant group. Sixty-one percent of Mexican immigrants have not graduated from high school, according to the 2006 census. Lacking education, they arrive poor and they usually stay poor. In fact, 41.4 percent of all post-1980 immigrants have remained poor a decade after they settled in the United States. Back in 1960, immigrants were much *less* likely to remain poor than the native-born; today, immigrants are much *more* likely to remain poor than natives.[17]

Politicians often draw a sharp line between legal and illegal immigration. But the 700,000 to 900,000 immigrants annually granted legal status raise many of the same concerns about the American future as their illegal counterparts. Because American immigration policy strongly favors family unification, new legal immigrants tend to be drawn overwhelmingly from the immediate relatives of recently naturalized Americans—many of whom started as illegals themselves. And the relatives of uneducated illegal immigrants usually lack education themselves.

This huge expansion of America's unskilled labor pool explains much of the trend toward inequality in the United States since 1970. It helps explain, too, why the median income has stagnated: It's hard for the average standard of living to rise when the country keeps doubling and redoubling its population of poor.

Most American policy makers shrug off the difficulties of these first-generation migrants. Migrants may stay poor, but they are still better off than they would have been had they stayed home.

Two considerations, however, should give us pause. First, poor migrants cost the taxpayer a great deal of money. The average Mexican immigrant collects over his or her lifetime $55,000 more in benefits than he or she pays in taxes.[18] And remember: Half these migrants are illegal and thus do not qualify for benefits like food stamps, Section 8 housing, Medicaid, and so on. The "earned legalization" proposed by President Bush and supported by many senators would qualify up to 12 million illegals for all these expensive programs. Most studies suggest that modern immigration delivers virtually zero net benefits to native-born Americans. Almost all the economic surplus created by immigration is captured by the migrants themselves.[19] In exchange for virtually zero economic benefits, native-born Americans must pay substantially higher taxes on account of immigration. In California alone, illegal immigration imposed a net cost of $10.5 billion upon state taxpayers in 2000,[20] or $1,183 for each household headed by a native-born American. That number would be still higher if the state had taken into account the far higher cost to the state treasury of *all* low-wage immigrants, those who have legalized themselves as well as those who have not.

Second, and even more troubling, evidence is rapidly accumulating that the poverty of the first generation of Hispanic immigrants will persist into the second and third generations. A first-generation Mexican-American earns on average about 40 percent less than other Americans, white and black. The economic evidence suggests that about half that income gap will be closed in the second generation and another half will be closed by the third—meaning that we can expect the incomes of the grandchildren of today's Mexican-American migrants still to be lagging 10 percent behind the national average well into the twenty-second century.[21]

The slow upward mobility of the children of newcomers strongly implies that the United States has imported a multigenerational problem. Hispanic students suffer from educational deficits very nearly as serious as those affecting African-Americans. As early as the fourth grade, the average Hispanic youngster scores almost 10 percent lower than the average white youngster in math proficiency.[22] Hispanic youth are three times as likely as whites and twice as likely as African-Americans to drop out of high school. Barely half of all Hispanic Americans finish high school in four years.[23]

The data suggest many possible explanations for this worrying record.

1. We know that the children of single mothers do much worse in school than the children of married families. Despite the widespread assumption that Hispanic migrants hew to culturally conservative folkways, 45 percent of Hispanic children are born out of wedlock as compared to 24 percent of whites.[24]

2. Since the Coleman Report of 1965, we have known that the educational level of parents is the single most powerful determinative of the educational level of those parents' children. American immigration policy has welcomed tens of millions of unskilled laborers across the Rio Grande since 1970. American leaders did this with their eyes open. A critic once suggested to then-Governor Bush that the United States would do better to encourage immigration only by the highly skilled, not busboys, valet parkers, and chicken pluckers. The governor snapped: "Well, what if we need chicken pluckers?"

3. Many Mexican migrants feel deep reluctance to assimilate to the English language and American ways. While 82 percent of immigrants born in Europe believe that all immigrants should be expected to learn English, only 54 percent of Mexican migrants think so. And while 67 percent of non-Mexican immigrants, including non-Mexican Latinos, believe that public school classes should be taught in English only, only 51 percent of Mexicans think so.[25] Are parents who oppose the teaching of English in the schools likely to read to their children in English at home? To keep English-language books in the house? To enroll their children at the local library? These are the first steps toward reading mastery. Kids who miss those steps lag behind their peers for the rest of their lives. At

age seventeen, Hispanic youngsters score 10 percent lower than whites on the National Assessment of Educational Progress's reading test. That gap yawns as wide today as in 1980.[26]

The United States has invested heavily to educate the post-1980 newcomers. A 1982 Supreme Court decision requires local authorities to educate all immigrants, legal and illegal, equally with the native-born. By the 2001–2002 school year, the states were educating some 3.7 million non-native speakers of English—and the numbers have mushroomed since then. Consider the case of North Carolina, not historically an immigration magnet. Between 2000 and 2005, Hispanics (the majority of them illegal) accounted for 57 percent of school enrollment growth in North Carolina. Educating school-age illegal immigrants cost North Carolina an estimated $10 million in 1995; $210 million in 2005.[27]

If money were the only cost, perhaps the United States could pay it. But massive immigration disrupts the education of the native-born as well. The commissioner of education for a North Carolina county with a fast-rising immigrant population told the local paper: "There is an impact on each family who has a kid in school. There is overcrowding and time taken away from their kids to try to get the non-English-speaking kids up to speed."[28]

In 2004, the online journal Education News conducted a wider survey of schoolteachers in immigration-heavy districts:

> Many of these kids come to kindergarten ill-prepared. . . . Most have no school experience whatsoever; their hands shake when they hold a pencil or crayon for the first time because they haven't developed their small motor skills, and they don't know how to use a pair of scissors. They don't know how to tie their shoes, name colors, any letters, or how to count to ten. . . .

It's hard to teach kids who sleep on the floor in a crowded apartment while older siblings watch TV or babies are howling. . . . Some have chronic health conditions that aren't treated . . .

We have to spend so much time on basic reading/writing/math skills that kids are seriously lacking in science and social studies backgrounds. . . . Gifted kids have to sit patiently in school while we hash and rehash out the same old skills, over and over, to the slow learners.[29]

With enough money, effort, and time, American schools may be able to impart to these children many of the skills they will need to make their way in an advanced society. But understand: We are talking about *a lot* of money, effort, and time—multiple generations. In order to have our chickens plucked in America, rather than import them preplucked from Mexico or Brazil, the American nation has assumed a vast and protracted commitment to tens of millions of people—over and on top of the as-yet-unfulfilled debt owed to those who still carry the wounds of slavery and segregation.

Every other country in the world seems to understand that economic policy must be founded on population policy. Canada and Australia have adopted immigration policies designed to attract the world's most highly skilled people. Japan and Germany have invested heavily in the steady improvement of the skills of the indigenous population. Even China's historically low skill levels are rising. In 1975, only 5 percent of Chinese students received any kind of secondary education. As of 2003, 44 percent of Chinese teenagers were receiving secondary education, and 17 percent of Chinese young people were continuing on to receive higher education.[30]

By contrast, only 70 percent of Americans graduate from high school—and even many of those graduates lack the math and literacy skills necessary to thrive in the modern world. In February 2007, the Educational Testing Service—the administrators of the SAT—warned of a sharp coming decline in the competence of the American workforce:

> We estimate that by 2030, the average levels of literacy and numeracy in the working-age population will have decreased by about 5%. . . . [O]ver the next 25 years or so, as better-educated individuals leave the workforce they will be replaced by those who, on average, have lower levels of education and skill.[31]

In 1992, Bill Clinton promised to "put people first." Republican and conservative economic policy should follow the old rogue's advice. If America is to flourish in this new century, the skill and qualifications of the American people must become our first economic priority. How?

Step One: Shut Down Racial Preferences

In the middle and late 1990s, the racial preference system built in the 1960s and 1970s came under attack. The state of California adopted a voter initiative to ban all preferences in 1996. Washington State followed in 1998. In 1996, the federal court of appeal for the fifth circuit struck down the University of Texas's affirmative action scheme as unconstitutional in *Hopwood v. Texas*—a case that the U.S. Supreme Court declined to overrule. California businessman Ward Connerly, the leader of the antiquota fight, announced that he would try to place a preferences ban on the ballot in Florida in 2000. In 1999, there seemed every reason to hope that the nation's three largest states would soon return to the race neutrality that most Americans had always assumed to be the goal of the civil rights movement.

That momentum was broken by the Bush presidency. The Bush family had never made any secret of its dislike and scorn for Connerly. As Governor Jeb Bush's press aide, Nicolle Devenish, put it when Connerly came to Florida, "While the governor is opposed to quotas and set-asides, we don't want to have a divisive political debate waged at a time when the governor's priority is improving schools and improving the lives of children, the elderly and the developmentally disabled."[32] Jeb Bush skillfully maneuvered to keep Connerly's initiative off the Florida ballot. In Texas, George W. Bush sought to evade *Hopwood* by requiring state universities to offer access to every student who finished in the top 10 percent of his high school class, regardless of that student's own actual test scores. Jeb went one better than George, announcing the same deal for the top 20 percent of every high school class, again regardless of those students' merits. In the 1980s, conservatives had deplored "race norming"—the practice of comparing white students only to other white students, black students only to other blacks. The Bush brothers cunningly repackaged de-facto race norming as an alternative to quotas. Students who attended predominantly Hispanic or black high schools would be compared only to other Hispanics or blacks. Their test scores—the one objective gauge of students' knowledge and learning potential—would be disregarded altogether.

The motive for this new policy was obvious: to keep off the Florida ballot in 2000 a ballot measure that might excite higher minority voter turnout and damage George W. Bush's presidential chances. As president, George W. Bush continued to support racial preferences in hiring and contracting.

President Bush personally decided that the United States government would intervene to defend preferences in the landmark *Grutter v. Bollinger* and *Gratz v. Bollinger* cases of 2003. In the *Grutter* case, the University of Michigan's own records showed that a black or Hispanic applicant with the same LSAT score as rejected applicant

Barbara Grutter would have been ten times as likely to be admitted to the University of Michigan Law School as a white or Asian applicant. Jennifer Gratz was rejected from the University of Michigan's undergraduate college by an admissions procedure that awarded 1 point for a well-written application essay and 20 points for membership in an approved race.

The Bush administration brief opposed the heavy-handed quota system at issue in *Grutter,* but argued for preserving the larger system of racial preferences challenged in *Gratz.*

And the President practiced what he preached! Introducing Hispanic Heritage Month at the White House in October 2001, the President ticked off his Hispanic hires with cringe-making gusto: "I thank our Attorney General for serving the country. I thank the Secretary of Commerce, Carlos Gutierrez, for serving the country. They're in my Cabinet. These are men who serve at the highest councils of government and can walk in the Oval Office any time they feel like it and say, 'Mr. President, here is what's on my mind.'"[33]

What did this departure from past Republican principle avail the administration? Very little. Bush received less than 10 percent of the black vote in 2000 and 2004. Republican congressional candidates performed equally dismally in 2002 and 2006. Bush attracted only about one-third of the Latino vote in 2000 and 2004[34]—less than Ronald Reagan received in 1980 and 1984. In the most important Latino state, California, Bush won barely one-fifth of the Hispanic vote.

When all else fails, it is time to try rethink. Racial preferences have seduced America's most talented minority students away from the study choices they need to make to succeed in life. Some argue that America's legacy of racial oppression explains the poor academic performance of so many minority students. But even if that were true, it would be a useless truth. Past discrimination may have caused the problem. Only hard work by students and parents in the here and now can *solve* the problem. Instead, racial preferences encourage everyone involved—students, parents, teachers, administrators—to game the system rather than do the work.

Preferring the underqualified over the qualified does the underqualified no favors, a point dramatized by new data from the nation's law schools.

- A majority of black law students graduate in the bottom tenth of their class; two-thirds of black students graduate in the bottom fifth of their class.

- Blacks are twice as likely to drop out of law school as whites.

- Only 45 percent of black law school graduates pass the bar on their first try, compared with 80 percent of white grads.

- Black law students are six times as likely to fail the bar even after multiple efforts.[35]

. These are very smart people we are talking about, people capable of great things. All Americans are poorer for their losses and defeats. The country is deprived of the talents they and students like them would have developed if only somebody had told them the truth early about how hard they would have to work and how much they needed to know.

Sometimes, of course, the underprepared get away with it. The affirmative action escalator whisks them along from a college for which they are not prepared to a corporate job for which they are not prepared to some high-level position for which they are not prepared . . . possibly even Attorney General of the United States, just to pluck an example out of thin air. In those cases, the costs of placing the wrong person in the wrong job are borne by the whole society. As the world gets more competitive, it becomes more urgent for America always to field its best possible teams, trained to the highest possible excellence, with no exceptions and no excuses.

In her opinion for the majority in *Grutter,* Justice Sandra Day O'Connor suggested that racial preferences should expire at some future point: She suggested twenty-five years from the date of writing. That would be 2028—a little remote from the present day, but still a fine opening bid. It is time for Republicans to reassert their fundamental belief in a single standard for all Americans: one nation, "e pluribus unum." The United States needs a national version of Ward Connerly's California Civil Rights Initiative, outlawing racial preferences in all areas of federal jurisdiction. The Republican Party came into being to champion equal justice under law against Democratic racialism. It is long past time for Republicans to return to the fight.

Step Two: Curtail Illegal Immigration—and Revise Legal Immigration to Favor Skilled over Unskilled Labor

American leaders today treat illegal immigration the way they once treated crime and, before that, inflation: as an unfortunate but easily exaggerated problem about which nothing much can be done. When President Bush pressed his amnesty-in-all-but-name proposals, he won the backing of virtually every prominent politician in both parties, as well as much of the business community. Even supposed opponents of his plan, like the conservative Indiana congressman Mike Pence, produced alternatives that amounted to amnesty on slightly different terms.

As opposition gathered to the President's plan, the administration launched a series of high-profile immigration raids. The administration may have hoped to allay conservative qualms about its lax enforcement record. On the other hand, the administration may have hoped to jolt business leaders into action by frightening them with a vision of endless harassment unless amnesty got passed. Or, possibly, both.

Certainly, the raids seem to have left behind the idea that the only alternative to some kind of amnesty would be a draconian program of raids and deportations. As Senator John McCain argued in favor of his McCain-Kennedy legislation:

> The reality is, 11 million people are not going to voluntarily come out of the shadows just to be shipped home. "Report to Deport" is not reality and it isn't workable. Systematically rounding up every person living here illegally and sending them home isn't a viable solution either. It is neither practically possible nor economically feasible. In fact, a recent study estimated that a mass deportation of the current undocumented would cost the federal government between $206 billion and $230 billion and that estimate assumes that several million will come forward voluntarily.[36]

Posing false alternatives like this is the oldest trick in bureaucratic politics. Henry Kissinger often joked about the State Department's genius for producing option papers that offered the president three choices: (1) do nothing; (2) wage global thermonuclear war; or (3) adopt the preferred State Department view. Likewise, limiting the range of options to deportation or amnesty overlooks the most effective response of all to the illegal immigration problem: voluntary compliance with the law by immigrants and employers.

Mark Krikorian of the Center for Immigration Studies observes that after 9/11, the immigration authorities deported some 1,500 Pakistani illegals. In the ensuing weeks, another 15,000 Pakistani migrants hastily departed the United States without any government action at all. Migration responds to market signals, and warnings that enforcement action may come raises the cost of illegality to migrant and employer alike.

It's a good guess that about 5 percent of the total U.S. labor force is made up of illegal aliens. That figure implies that somewhere between 2.5 million and 3 million illegals get hired each and every year in the United States.[37] If better enforcement complicated those transactions even slightly, it could greatly alter the incentives facing both migrants and employers. And since probably 1.5 million of the illegals have resided in the United States for less than twenty-four months—and 3 million for less than forty-eight months—even a small alteration of their economic incentives could induce many of these lightly rooted illegals to return home, without raids and without deportations. One expert estimates that moderate enforcement provisions could cut the illegal population in half over the next half-decade, at a cost of less than $2 billion over five years.[38]

Many conservatives have made a border fence a test of seriousness on the migration issue. You can well understand their frustration when not only their government, but their own political party, shrug off their concerns—and when indeed the president they supported through two elections dismisses their views as bigoted and unworthy of discussion.

But the hard fact is that a migration fence will take far longer to build than most conservatives appreciate—and will cost much more. It required almost a decade of litigation to complete the fourteen-mile fence that now separates San Diego from Tijuana. (Opponents charged that the fence would threaten a wetland on the Pacific Ocean.) A border fence may help a little to slow the influx of future illegals. But it will obviously do nothing about illegals already here—and already benefiting from America's ollee-ollee-oxenfree policy, which invests billions to guard the border while doing almost nothing to enforce the law inside the country. Real enforcement begins with offering employers a reliable database of legal workers and a convenient way to check job applicants against that database. Those employers who hire nonlegals should face severe financial sanctions, comparable to those levied on violators of the Clean Water Act: up to $25,000 per day per offense.

The next Republican president should address the problem of immigration as a whole. Immigration should be used to enhance the skill level of the U.S. workforce, not (as at present) to degrade it. Stricter limits should be placed on the total number of family-reunification visas. Within the family-reunification category, preference should be given to those families that can demonstrate they have never applied for government assistance. The number of visas for skilled labor should be increased, especially for the most skilled workers. The United States should imitate Canada's point system, which gives preference to workers who hold advanced degrees, who speak English fluently, who are younger than forty-nine, who have a job waiting for them, and whose spouses also are educated.

With all due respect to Governor George Bush's concerns for the chicken-plucking industry, it is a bad bargain to buy cheaper chicken today at the expense of declining national skill and wealth for generations to come. And with all due respect to the political leaders who have lined up to endorse one form or another of amnesty, it is an even worse bargain for Republicans to jettison their claims to represent the broad interests of the nation in pursuit of votes we will not get and campaign donations of which we already have more than enough.

The security and stability of Mexico rank, of course, as supreme American interests. One of the most important, but seldom declared, motives for America's lax immigration policy has been to provide a safety valve for Mexico's troubled economy and potentially revolutionary society. It's not a coincidence that the great wave of migration from Mexico commenced—was allowed to commence—in the late 1970s, as Central America was plunging into civil war. The prospect of an El Salvador–like conflict on America's southern border understandably terrified policy makers. Allowing the ambitious and disaffected to escape Mexico must have seemed to many a more practical alternative to reform or repression. But three decades later, we have reached the point where one out of every five living Mexican-born people now resides in the United States, a population extrusion unmatched since the Irish potato famine. Accepting these migrants as permanent lawful residents of the United States entails accepting a vast, difficult multigenerational responsibility without any strong surety of success.

Step Three: Support Larger Families

High immigration levels are often justified as necessary to save the United States from the demographic doom that seems to threaten the welfare states of Western Europe. The United States has promised substantial benefits to its retirees, and those have to be paid by taxes on younger workers. Since American birth rates have slipped below replacement—2.0 per woman, with the fertility rates for African-American women and non-Hispanic white women even lower still—immigration is advertised as the country's only hope for paying its obligations.

But fertility rates respond to economic conditions and public policy. The Republican Congress of the 1990s introduced a $500-per-child tax credit. President Bush's 2001 tax cut increased that credit to $1,000. Look what happened next: Fertility rates rose in the late 1990s and remained high even during the economically more stressful years after 2001. This should come as no surprise: A gathering body of evidence suggests that carefully designed tax benefits do promote childbearing.[39] That makes intuitive sense. Meanwhile, overgenerous social security systems (like those prevailing in Western Europe) have been shown to discourage childbearing, probably because the payroll taxes used in most countries to finance social security systems fall most heavily on people in their peak childbearing years.[40]

Even in the straitened fiscal circumstances ahead, Republicans should and must fight to defend and increase the pro-family tax policies introduced in the 1990s. In fact, we should be trying to improve them.

The $1,000-per-child tax credit should be indexed to inflation to preserve its value in the years ahead.

We want the credit to remain lucrative. But even more, we should want to ensure that it remains available to all parents—not just a few lucky families whose incomes land in a particular tax bracket.

The dirty secret of Bush tax policy was that it extended the full child credit to surprisingly few people. Remember, the credit only offset income-tax liability. Many lower-income families paid only or mostly payroll taxes even before 2001—and so had little or no taxable income for the credit offset.

Meanwhile, as mentioned above, professional and upper-middle-income families also lost the benefit of the per-child tax credit to the alternative minimum tax.

Our Republican and conservative tax policy should encourage childbearing by extending the full benefits of the per-child tax credit to *all* parents. If we credited the per-child benefit against payroll taxes too, we would extend its fullest benefit to lower-income parents. We should also exempt the benefit from being clawed back by the alternative minimum tax, so as to encourage upper-middle-income people to consider having that third or fourth child. That will strengthen America, reduce the seeming need for unskilled immigration—and, by the way, restore our Republican reputation as the champions of family and parenthood.

The United States should continue to welcome a moderate level of orderly, legal, and highly skilled migration. But it should disembarrass itself of the dangerous idea that migration could or should substitute for bearing and raising our own children. Immigration is to fertility what wine is to food: delightful as a complement; deadly as a substitute.

SIX

GOAL THREE:
New Life for the Pro-Life

Here's a test of your moral intuitions: Which of the following scenarios troubles you more?

1. A teenage girl from a low-income, single-parent family finds herself pregnant. The pregnancy threatens all her ambitions in life. The father of the baby makes plain he will not marry her—and anyway, he has few immediate prospects himself either. The thought of abandoning a child to a big-city foster care program terrifies her. Ten weeks into her pregnancy, she has an abortion.

2. A major pharmaceutical company discovers evidence that embryonic stem cells have the potential to offer cures for a rare disease. It buys dozens of eight-day-old frozen fertilized embryos from fertility clinics in the United Kingdom. The company extracts the stem cells for research, terminating these embryos' potential for life.

My own personal answer is #2. I can sympathize with a frightened girl searching for the best decision available to her under huge, life-altering pressures. But killing dozens of potential human beings for research purposes—that revolts me. However, all the evidence tells me I am pretty much alone in that view. While abortion remains bitterly morally contested in the United States, the public overwhelmingly favors embryo-killing research.

Most pollsters flinch from using phrases like "embryo-killing." They ask about "tissues taken from human embryos," leaving behind an impression that we are dealing with something like a biopsy or a DNA swab.

In a rare departure from the mealymouthed rule, Peter Hart and Robert Teeter posed the question more directly in June 2004, in a poll for NBC News.

> There is a type of medical research that involves using special cells, called stem cells, that are obtained from human embryos. These human embryo stem cells are then used to generate new cells and tissue that could help treat or cure many diseases. I am now going to read you two statements about this type of research.
>
> Statement A: Those OPPOSED to this type of research say that it crosses an ethical line by using cells from potentially viable human embryos, when this research can be done on animals or by using other types of cells.
>
> Statement B: Those IN FAVOR of this research say that it could lead to breakthrough cures for many diseases, such as cancer, Alzheimer's, Parkinson's, and spinal cord injuries, and this research uses only embryos that otherwise would be discarded.

That question frames the issue as starkly as it has ever been framed. And the results could not be more emphatic. Of those surveyed, 71 percent said they favor such research and 22 percent oppose it.[1] That is what is called in the trade a landslide.

Nobody respects a landslide more than a working politician. Who wants to face ads like this, unleashed against Missouri Republican senator Jim Talent in 2006?

Shaky from Parkinson's but still boyishly handsome, the movie star Michael Fox speaks directly to the camera.

As you may know, I care deeply about the issue of stem-cell research.

In Missouri, you can elect Claire McCaskill [smile], who shares my hope for cures.

Unfortunately, Senator Jim Talent opposes expanding stem-cell research. Senator Talent even wants [catch in voice] to criminalize the science that gives us a chance for hope.

They say all politics is local, but that's not always the case. What you do in Missouruh [using the pronunciation favored in the Republican areas of the state] matters to millions of Americans. [sad pause] Americans like me. [fade to black][2]

McCaskill's market researchers claimed this one ad made Republicans 10 percent more likely to vote for McCaskill. If true, that would make the Fox ad one of the most devastatingly effective political ads of the 2000s, far more effective even than the Swiftboat ads against Senator John Kerry. Whatever the poll numbers, there's no arguing the final tally: In 2006, Missouri—the home state of Phyllis Schlafly and John Ashcroft, one of the most pro-life states in the union—voted 51.2 percent to 48.8 percent to amend their state constitution to guarantee the right to conduct embryonic stem-cell research. Missourians defeated incumbent senator Jim Talent and elected Democrat Claire McCaskill, the first living Democrat to win a senatorial election in Missouri since 1982.[3]

In more liberal states, stem-cell research proved an even more powerful issue. In 2004, Californians were still digging out from the disaster of their energy crisis. The crisis had piled tens of billions of dollars of deeply resented debts onto state taxpayers. Yet in November 2004, only thirteen months after Californians recalled Governor Gray Davis, they voted 59 percent to 41 percent in favor of a $3 billion bond issue to finance a state stem-cell research fund, joining Connecticut, Illinois, Maryland, Massachusetts, and New Jersey, which had previously created similar state funds.

You would not know from this barrage that President Bush had in fact *approved* embryonic stem-cell research back in 2001. The executive orders he issued that summer allowed universities, corporations, foundations, and state governments to experiment upon human embryos without limit or restraint. The only restriction he imposed was a restriction on federal research dollars: Those could be used only for experiments upon embryos already terminated.

Yet even this tentative step may have been a step too far. Polls consistently find that Americans favor full federal funding of stem-cell research by margins of 60 percent to 30 percent. Republicans should brace themselves for a vigorous Democratic campaign on the issue in the years ahead.

Democrats will use the issue with special avidity because stem-cell research is supported most strongly by groups that Republicans most desperately need to win. White Catholics favor full federal funding of embryonic stem-cell research by a margin of 60 percent to 32 percent. Embryonic stem-cell research is supported strongly by moderates and independents—and even by 39 percent of those who wish to see abortion made illegal.[4]

I used to believe that the advent of new biological technologies would open a new era of political controversy in the United States. This prediction has thus far proven utterly wrong. To the extent that they think about them at all, Americans seem to accept almost all of these new possibilities with surprising equanimity—or anyway, indifference.

Sometimes acceptance comes after a short delay. In 1980, hundreds of pro-life activists protested the opening of the nation's first in-vitro fertilization clinic in Norfolk, Virginia. Just as with embryonic stem-cell research, the pro-life movement persuaded the federal government to deny federal research dollars to the new industry. And as will likely prove the case with embryonic stem cells, the denial of federal money made not a whit of difference. Today, more than 1 million Americans seek fertility treatments every year from hundreds of clinics. Reproduction doctors can offer families ever more sophisticated services. Some innovations may raise the national eyebrow for a day or two—but qualms over yesterday's taboo-bursting are rapidly left behind as new possibilities zoom upon us. In 1991, a South Dakota woman carried to term a baby conceived from her daughter's egg and her son-in-law's sperm—and was rewarded with a heartwarming portrayal in the made-for-TV movie *The Arlette Schweitzer Story.*

Surrogate motherhood—hiring a woman to bear a pregnancy formed from another woman's eggs—once excited enough unease for two states, New York and Michigan, to ban the practice outright. In 1993, however, California courts upheld the validity of surrogacy contracts. California's decision created some tricky new legal dilemmas. For example, in 1995 an infertile couple in Santa Ana, California, hired a surrogate mother to carry a child created from a sperm and egg purchased from anonymous donors. One month before the child's birth, the Santa Ana husband filed for divorce. He argued that he should not have to pay support for the expected baby since his ex-wife was not the child's "mother." The California courts had to sort out which of the child's five potential parents should be regarded as the "father" and the "mother." (After protracted litigation, the husband lost.)[5] But difficulties like this have not led any considerable number of Americans to express doubts about surrogacy. Instead, the business has gone international, with more and more American would-be parents preferring Third World (especially Indian) surrogates as cheaper and less litigious than their American counterparts.

In 2000, a Colorado couple received the terrible news that their six-year-old daughter suffered from a rare and fatal bone-marrow disease that could kill her unless she received a bone-marrow dona-tion from someone with the identical tissue type. The couple fertil-ized fifteen eggs. One of the ensuing embryos made a genetic match. The couple carried that one to birth. The transplant was done and the elder child saved. The fourteen embryos that did not match were discarded.[6] Who would dare criticize? Who would do any-thing different? Yet if we are discarding potential human lives be-cause they do not meet a predetermined medical standard, what happens as that medical standard shifts? As we gain the ability to detect which embryos will be prone to mental illness and which to low IQ, which to violent temper and which to physical ugliness, which to hypertension and which to obesity, which to homosexual-ity and which to autism? On the record, the answer seems to be: As we gain these abilities, we will use them.

President Bush tried a second time to set some moral limits on biological science in 2006. In his State of the Union address that year, he asked Congress to ban the purchase and sale of human embryos, to forbid human cloning, and to outlaw human-animal hybrids. Congress did not respond, and not because of pressure from the mermaid-and-centaur lobby. An American laboratory had al-ready created a part-human, part-cow embryo for research purposes as far back as 1998. The next year, two biotech companies success-fully introduced one human gene into the embryo of a calf, produc-ing a transgenic cow whose milk contained more humanlike proteins. Nobody objected, and if further hybridization offers sub-stantial health and commercial advantages, it seems unlikely that anybody will object to those experiments either.

Nothing in recent years has more sharply delimited the power of the pro-life movement than the Terri Schiavo controversy. The fate of this severely impaired woman convulsed the Congress in 2005. Florida courts had approved petitions by Schiavo's husband and legal guardian to turn off her feeding tube. Florida governor Jeb Bush and Republicans in Congress led by Senate Majority Leader Bill Frist intervened to restore feeding. The courts dismissed all these interventions, and Schiavo expired on March 31, 2005.

In retrospect, the Schiavo case looks like the first warning of the series of disasters and debacles that would befall the Republican Party in 2005–2006: Katrina, the Harriet Miers nomination, the failed immigration amnesty, the attack on the Golden Dome of Samarra that triggered a wave of anti-Sunni militia violence in Iraq, the Abramoff scandals, and all the rest. By a margin of 70 percent to 27 percent, Americans repudiated Congress's intervention in the matter. They supported her husband's decision to remove Schiavo's feeding tube 63 percent to 28 percent. More than 15 percent of those surveyed said they had been involved in a similar decision for a friend or relative—and it was these Americans who reacted most vehemently against Congress's actions.[7]

Inspired by Pope John Paul II's 1995 encyclical *Evangelium Vitae,* many in the pro-life movement had hoped to broaden their message. In the pope's words, "With the new prospects opened up by scientific and technological progress there arise new forms of attacks on the dignity of the human being,"[8] above and beyond abortion itself. Pro-lifers began to talk about a "culture of life" that might possibly include issues from reproductive technology to genocide in Darfur to better working conditions for Third World laborers. Those hopes, I think it is fair to say, have been disappointed.

So long as the pro-life movement addressed abortion and only abortion, it wielded tremendous power in American politics. True, pro-choice Americans outnumber pro-life Americans. But pro-lifers care about abortion a lot more than pro-choicers do. About 12 percent of Americans tell pollsters they regard abortion as one of their top one or two voting issues. That 12 percent voted 45–35 for Bob Dole in 1996 and 2–1 for Republican candidates for Congress in 1994.[9] The swing voters coveted by politicians are much more likely to be pro-life than pro-choice. Women are more likely to be pro-life than men; Ohioans more than New Yorkers; high school graduates more than Ph.D.s.

For these voters, the abortion issue is much more than a philosophical debate about human personhood. It is a direct challenge to their dearest beliefs about sexuality, family, and the meaning of life.

When the abortion rights movement exploded upon 1970s America, it delighted in shock and offense. "If men got pregnant, abortion would be a sacrament," went one slogan from 1973, and many in the abortion rights movement spoke as if pregnancy and children represented a threat to women's freedom and social progress.

Against this gleeful perversity, the pro-life movement rallied millions of conservative Americans. Between 1976 and 1980, the abortion issue helped shift dozens of congressional and senatorial seats away from the Democrats toward the GOP. Among the trophies on the pro-lifers' wall:

1976: Vance Hartke (Indiana); Joseph Montoya (New Mexico); Frank Moss (Utah); Stuart Symington (Missouri); and John Tunney (California)

1978: James Abourezk (South Dakota—forced into retirement rather than face defeat); Wendell Anderson (Minnesota); Dick Clark (Iowa); Floyd Haskell (Colorado); and Thomas McIntyre (New Hampshire)

1980: Birch Bayh (Indiana); John Culver (Iowa); Frank Church (Idaho); Mike Gravel (Alaska); Warren Magnuson (Washington);

George McGovern (South Dakota); Robert Morgan (North Carolina); Gaylord Nelson (Wisconsin); Richard Stone (Florida)

Since 1976, the pro-life movement has undergirded the Republicans' credibility as the party of decent, traditional, religious Americans.

Millions of Americans perceived abortion as the poisoned tip of
a dagger that threatened everything they held dear. As these voters
saw it, the abortion movement denigrated the worth of wives and
mothers. It threatened the authority of parents over children. And—
most lethally—it seemed determined to tempt girls into potentially
life-wrecking sexual irresponsibility.

Legal abortion arrived in the United States at the same time as
dramatic changes in sexual and marital behavior. American women
took many more sex partners and married later—or not at all.
Attitudes toward children turned deeply hostile. It is really striking
how many of the movies of the 1970s feature evil, demonic, killer
children: *Rosemary's Baby, The Omen, The Exorcist, It's Alive!*

Some people experienced these changes as liberating. Many others experienced them as deeply threatening. For these latter, casual
abortion seemed to symbolize everything that had gone wrong in
modern America.

Over three decades, the ascendant pro-life movement has succeeded in setting limits on the excesses of abortion. They ended
Medicaid funding of abortion in 1976. (Today, government money
funds only 14 percent of American abortions.) They introduced
parental-notification rules for teenage abortion, compulsory counseling, and other limits. They discouraged hospitals and doctors from
practicing abortion in culturally conservative counties and states. By
the National Abortion Rights Action League's tally, some 383 laws
restrictive of abortion have been enacted by state legislatures between
1995 and 2006. Most of these laws have survived judicial scrutiny.[10]

The pro-life movement has tipped the courts away from their past unyielding defense of abortion in even its most extreme and outrageous forms. In the 2000 case of *Steinberg v. Carhart,* the Supreme Court ruled 5–4 that states could not ban partial-birth-abortion techniques. In April 2007, the Supreme Court reversed itself and allowed a new ban on the procedure to stand. The 2007 majority included the two Bush-appointed justices, John Roberts and Samuel Alito. But perhaps even more important than the change in the court was the change in the country. In 2000, the court struck down a law passed by Nebraska's single-chamber state. The ban upheld in 2007 had been enacted by both houses of Congress in 2003, with favorable votes from 17 Democratic senators (including future majority leader Harry Reid) and 63 Democratic members of the House of Representatives. The 2003 ban had been backed by 65 percent of Americans surveyed. More liberal jurists often invoke the concept of "evolving standards of decency" to justify overturning old precedents. Such an evolution of standards seems exactly to have occurred between 2000 and 2007.

Above all, the pro-life movement has compelled liberal and Democratic politicians to stop exulting over abortion as an act of liberation. As recently as 1992, Bill Clinton declared himself "strongly" pro-choice when he accepted the Democratic presidential nomination. In 2004, John Kerry declined to mention the subject. The previous month, Kerry—a senator with a 100 percent pro-choice voting record—told the *Washington Post*: "I oppose abortion, personally. I don't like abortion. I believe life does begin at conception."[11] Hillary Clinton, the Democratic front-runner for 2008, describes abortion as "sad, even tragic."[12]

Yet, as often happens in politics, the past success of the pro-life movement has changed society in ways that make further successes increasingly difficult.

- American women are having fewer abortions. Over the twenty years from 1981 to 2001, the incidence of abortion among women of childbearing age (15–44) declined by almost 33 percent, from 29.3 abortions per 1,000 women to 21.1.[13] In 2002, the total number of abortions conducted in the United States dropped beneath 1.3 million, the lowest figure since 1976. And there it has stayed.

- *Roe* or no *Roe,* America is gradually reaching a compromise whereby abortion is available in liberal states and unavailable in conservative ones. The number of abortion providers declined nationwide by 11 percent between 1996 and 2000. No legal abortions at all were performed in 87 percent of U.S. counties.

- America has likewise groped its way to a consensus against late abortion and against easy access to abortion for teenagers. Nine out of ten abortions in the United States now take place in the first twelve weeks of pregnancy. More than 80 percent of the women who undergo abortion are legal adults.

- Increasingly, abortion is concentrated among women for whom childbearing would truly represent a hardship. Between 1992 and 2002, the incidence of abortion decreased 20 percent among higher-income women, while increasing 29 percent among lower-income women.[14] The large majority of abortions, more than 60 percent, occur among women who already have at least one child.

In the face of these facts, it is difficult to see where the pro-life movement can go from here. Assuming that the Democrats avoid the foolish, provocative mistakes of the past, the abortion right will contract into the form supported by two-thirds of American voters: an emergency option available to adult women in dire need, provided that local majorities do not object too much. Not a logical result, certainly not morally clear-cut, but one that will likely prove amazingly politically stable.

Attempts through the political process to shrink the abortion right beyond that point will almost certainly call forth a pro-choice backlash in exactly the same way that *Roe v. Wade* summoned up the pro-life movement.

That is not a hypothetical statement. Look at the events of 2006 in South Dakota, probably the most pro-life state in the union. In January, the South Dakota legislature passed the most stringent abortion ban ever contemplated in American law. The law was purely symbolic, of course, so long as *Roe v. Wade* remained valid. But should *Roe* ever be overturned, state law would take effect— and in South Dakota that would mean an absolute ban on abortion except to save the life of the mother, without even a rape or incest exception. Doctors who performed abortions would face sentences of up to ten years in prison.

The law galvanized South Dakota Democrats to place a repeal motion on the November ballot. It passed by a margin of 8 to 1.

More such defeats probably await the pro-life movement in the future—and worse.

It portends something, I suspect, that two of the three 2008 Republican front-runners, Rudy Giuliani and Mitt Romney, lacked plausible pro-life credentials—and that the sincerity of the third, John McCain, was widely doubted. The pro-life movement found itself gravitating to second-tier no-hopers (Huckabee, Brownback) or to wild-card candidates years removed from elective office (Gingrich, Thompson).

It portends something too that so many rank-and-file Republicans proved willing to subordinate the abortion issue when shopping for their 2008 candidates. True, Giuliani and Romney each in their way deferred to pro-life sensibilities. But the level of deference these candidates offered in 2008 would have been rejected as utterly inadequate in, say, 1988.

Rank-and-file Republicans seem already to have intuited what the leaders of the pro-life movement will probably acknowledge only after years of harsh negative experience: The pro-life cause in the twenty-first century will look very like the temperance movement after the repeal of Prohibition. It will emphasize education and persuasion rather than coercion, changes in attitudes and beliefs rather than changes in law and public policy.

Does that sound weak-willed? It should not. In fact, one of the greatest conservative triumphs of recent years has been the slow reversal of the sexual revolution of the 1970s, not by law but by experience.

On abortion, for example, most polls suggest that Americans shifted five points in a pro-life direction between 1990 and 2005[15]— the result, perhaps, of the spread of ultrasound photography and other images that have taught Americans how early the infant in the womb comes visibly to look recognizably human.

Americans have turned noticeably more conservative on divorce and premarital sex as well.

A majority of Americans, 59 percent, think divorce should be more difficult to get than it currently is.[16] Americans who witnessed the divorce upsurge of the 1970s as children resist divorce for themselves: People born after 1955 are much less likely to divorce than people born before 1955. (The most divorce-prone cohort: people born between 1942 and 1951.)[17]

The decline in the national abortion rate has been driven in large part by a decline in sexual activity among teenagers. Between 1993 and 2003, the percentage of young people who had engaged in sexual intercourse before graduating from high school dropped from 53 percent to 47 percent. The percentage of high school students who slept around a lot in high school dropped even more steeply. In 1993, 19 percent of high schoolers had engaged in sexual intercourse with four or more partners. In 2003, only 15 percent had done so.[18]

People learn!

On the other hand, some people learn faster than others.

The positive national trends toward fewer abortions, less divorce, and less promiscuity have been driven by changes at the top of society, among the best-educated Americans.

We saw earlier that the incidence of abortion has dropped radically among affluent women. Divorce has followed the same trend.

About 35 percent of the noncollege women who married in the late 1970s were divorced within their first ten years of marriage. The rate of divorce among similarly educated women who married in the early 1990s? Almost exactly the same.

Now look at what has happened among the college-educated. Among college-educated women who married in the late 1970s, 27 percent divorced before their tenth anniversary. But among college-educated women who married in the early 1990s, only 16 percent divorced in the first ten years.

As a general rule, about two-thirds of divorces occur within the first ten years of marriage. Finish the math, and you see that over her lifetime, a non–college graduate who married in the early 1990s faces more than a 1-in-2 chance of divorce; a college graduate, less than a 1-in-4 chance.[19] That represents a stark difference in life outcomes for both women and their children.

And even these numbers radically understate the marriage gap between the highly educated and the less educated, the rich and the poor. Not only do the less educated divorce at higher rates, but they are less likely to get married in the first place. Only one-tenth of college-educated mothers were living without a husband in the year 2000, while 36 percent of noncollege mothers were living alone.[20] One-third of American children are born to unmarried women. But only 4 percent of college-educated women give birth unwed.[21]

The marital status of their parents has become the single most important determinant of the fate of America's children: more important than race, more important than poverty. In fact, it is marriage that determines whether a child grows up poor or not. Children in married families are dramatically less likely to suffer hardship than children in non-married families—*even when the married families earn precisely the same income as the nonmarried.*[22]

Children who grow up in a household different from that of their biological father face a radically more difficult future than children who grow up with their father. A child who grows up without his or her biological father in the home is twice as likely to drop out of high school as a child who grows up with his or her biological father.[23] Children living apart from their fathers get worse grades and score lower on standardized tests.[24] They are less likely to enroll in college or to graduate if enrolled.[25] After they finish school, they are less likely to work.[26] Girls who live without their biological fathers are 50 percent more likely to get pregnant in their teens than girls who live with their fathers.[27] Boys are more likely to get into trouble with the law and go to jail.[28] All these effects remain strong even if the single parent remarries and even if the family earns a middle-class income.

Author Kay Hymowitz worries that this marriage gap is "self-perpetuating" and threatening to harden America's already rising inequality into a true "caste society."[29]

For it is not only outcomes that are diverging between rich and poor, between the highly educated and the less educated: It is attitudes and values.

Non–college graduates are about 50 percent more likely than the college-educated to hold antimarriage attitudes, to agree that "marriage is an outmoded institution" or that "it is unrealistic to expect two people to remain married to one another for life."[30] College-educated Americans are more likely than the non–college-educated to agree that divorce harms children. They are more likely to disapprove of unmarried cohabitation.[31] And while they don't want to judge . . . still, they do frown on casual sex more strongly than their peers did two decades ago. Meanwhile, non–college-track Americans express the same acceptance of casual sex as they did when CB radio was the rage.[32]

Make no mistake, upper-class America has not reverted to the moral traditionalism of the past. But elite Americans have absorbed the practical lessons of the upheaval of the 1970s, backed by terabytes of data and research, that getting married and staying married hugely enhance their own and their children's welfare and well-being.

They have absorbed those lessons—but they hesitate to impart them.

At the same time that America's upper classes have stabilized their family lives, the American institutions and the American mass culture run by those upper classes continue to bombard everybody else with very different kinds of messages. If you learn about the world around you from daytime television and pop music and celebrity magazines, you would strongly be led to believe that unwed parenthood, hook-ups and split-ups, and nonmarital sexuality are not only norms but ideals. That's how the stars of TV, movie, music, and sports live, isn't it? Never mind that the executives, agents, accountants, lawyers, publicists, and all the rest who actually create and sustain the illusion of stardom are returning home at night to their families in Westchester or the Palisades, monitoring their children's homework, and dutifully writing you-never-know checks to their colleges' alumni funds.

These class issues form the undiscussed backdrop to the contentious debate over same-sex marriage.

As issues go, same-sex marriage may be the weirdest ever to inflame public passions. No question, same-sex marriage excites intense feelings. It has been battled in the courts and in political campaigns. A majority of the states, twenty-seven at last count, have amended their constitutions to prevent courts from foisting same-sex marriage upon them. Nineteen more have done the same through ordinary legislation. Meanwhile, a generation of gay activists have devoted themselves to same-sex marriage as the great civil rights issue of our time.

And yet, as a practical matter, same-sex marriage is not a right that seems much to interest its intended beneficiaries. In the first three years after the Massachusetts Supreme Judicial Council authorized same-sex marriages, only 6,500 Massachusetts couples took advantage of the new right. If we assume that 5 percent of the Massachusetts adult population is gay, slightly higher than the national average, then only about one-twentieth of the gay adult population of the state has used its hard-won new equality.

You see equal indifference whenever same-sex marriage is accepted into law. Same-sex marriages commenced in the Netherlands on April 1, 2001. As of the end of 2005, only 8,112 couples had used their new right,[33] fewer than 1 out of 25 adult Dutch homosexuals.

Norway recognized same-sex partnerships in 1994; as of 2004, it had registered only 1,808 partnerships.[34] Sweden authorized same-sex unions in 1995; between 1995 and 2002, Swedish couples registered only 1,526 same-sex partnerships.[35] Canadian, Danish, and Spanish gays have shown similarly wan enthusiasm for wedlock.

So what are we arguing about?

In his new book on the future of marriage, David Blankenhorn cites some worrying information from the International Social Survey Program. Pollsters asked respondents in forty countries whether they agreed or disagreed with six basic statements about marriage, three positive, three negative. (For example: "Married people are generally happier than unmarried people" and "One parent can bring up a child as well as two parents together.") Countries that recognize same-sex unions express far more antimarriage sentiment than do people in Australia and the United States, the two major democracies that do not.[36]

In other words: People accept same-sex marriage only to the extent that they have lost faith in marriage in general. Same-sex marriage is less a social revolution in its own right than a flashing indicator of a larger social change.

Most Republicans and conservatives oppose same-sex marriage. But they are understandably uncomfortable with the issue. Republicans and conservatives reject persecution and intolerance. Voters mistrust any group of politicians who seem overly interested in what Ralph Nader once dubbed "gonad politics." Americans, with characteristic decency, increasingly reject and condemn the sniggering cruelty with which homosexuals were treated in the past.

Whether because they accept claims of gay equality, or because they feel pity toward homosexuals as a persecuted group, or because they want the issue to go away, Americans have moved toward acceptance of same-sex marriage over the past dozen years. Massachusetts performs same-sex marriages. Connecticut, New Jersey, Vermont, and Washington all offer civil unions equivalent to marriage. (Washington's civil unions are available also to heterosexual couples.) California, Maine, the District of Columbia, and Hawaii have more restrictive civil union laws. Only a very bare majority of Americans opposed same-sex marriage in 2004, with opposition weaker among women than among men, and weakest of all among younger voters. Opposition has declined further in just the two years from 2004 to 2006. Conservatives will probably still hold a majority in the issue in 2008. But in 2012? 2016? 2020?

Even in 2004, the issue did Republicans little practical good. Of the five states where George Bush's share of the vote rose most between 2000 and 2004, not one had a same-sex-marriage initiative on the ballot. Of the ten states where Bush's vote share rose least, three had same-sex-marriage initiatives.[37] The claim that the same-sex-marriage issue tipped Ohio to Bush seems almost certainly wrong. Ohio was one of the states where Bush's vote increased the very least between 2000 and 2004.

It is dangerous for any party to be known as a party "against" something. The next Republican president has to make clear that when he or she opposes same-sex marriage, he or she does so because he or she stands *for* something: for the revival of marriage, for the family as the greatest social welfare institution we have, for an equal chance in life for all American children.

These intimate topics embarrass politicians, especially politicians with less than perfect personal lives themselves (that is—almost all of them). But if we do not find ways to address these topics, we as conservatives will never be able to address issues of poverty and inequality. And those issues are becoming increasingly important to voters, as they should.

The Bush administration advanced a tentative marriage-promotion initiative through the Department of Health and Human Services, to little effect. The program funded voluntary marriage counseling for low-income couples. Unfortunately, there is little hard evidence that such marriage-education programs do any real good.

What's needed instead is a massive national education campaign to teach new norms. In January 2005, the Ad Council launched a national campaign to inform smoking parents of the risks their habit posed to their children:

> Children with at least one smoking parent have a 25–40% increased risk of chronic respiratory symptoms.
>
> Most Americans are not aware that the smoke trailing off the lit end of a cigarette is a toxic fog of gases including ammonia, carbon monoxide and hydrogen cyanide. And while this fog is harmful to all people, it is even more dangerous to children due to their smaller lung capacity. What's more, the majority of parents who smoke underestimate the effects of it on their children, and 54% do not have rules against smoking in the house. This campaign [seeks to] educate parents about the dangers of secondhand smoke and

motivate them to create smoke-free environments for their families.[38]

Fine. Good. When will we see an Ad Council campaign addressing the danger posed by out-of-wedlock child rearing? Kodak, Coca-Cola, and McDonald's have all sponsored contests offering prizes to students who write the best essays on the importance of staying in school. When will a major corporation offer a prize for the best essay on why young people should marry before having children? The American Library Association recruited Denzel Washington to pose for a poster with the single word "Read." When will somebody ask Washington—an unostentatiously devoted husband and father of four—to take a stance for marriage?

The majority of school family-life courses, now usually labeled "abstinence plus" so as to qualify for federal abstinence-education funding, avoid the whole area of the life outcomes for children of unwed mothers. America's classrooms are full of such kids, and very understandably nobody wants to make them feel bad. But should protecting their feelings really take priority over protecting the next generation?

There are obviously sharp and narrow limits upon the ability of government to change behavior. And yet there are things the next Republican president—and Republican governors and Republican legislators—can do.

1. Send to Congress a ban on all purchase and sale of fertilized human embryos. President Bush pitched his tent on the wrong ground when he set limits on embryo research—he sounded anti-science, anti-cure. Better to defend the clear and powerful principle that human life should not be bought and sold. After all: If the embryos cannot be bought and sold, the incentive for the research will disappear.

2. Make clear that Republicans understand and accept that the overturning of *Roe v. Wade* will leave behind different abortion laws in different states—that it is the Democrats who are the abortion extremists, not we.

3. Create an Office of Marriage and Children within the Office of Public Health, with a mandate to research the physical and mental public health benefits of marital stability—and to propose appropriate steps to sustain and strengthen marriage. Federal law and the law of most states currently ban discrimination on the basis of marital status. Those bans were inserted into the law in the late 1960s and early 1970s, in an attempt to ease the stigma that afflicted the unwed minority. A third of a century later, an absolute majority of American children will spend some portion of their lives in an unmarried family. Could there be a clearer measure of policy failure? It's time for America to reassert marriage as a norm, not only in policy, but in law.

4. Passing a national constitutional amendment defining marriage as the union of one man and one woman will likely prove impossible. Attempting it may well prove dangerous. Republicans need to be very clear what it is that we are concerned about: not the word "marriage," but the multiplication of quasimarital statuses, especially when those are opened to cohabiting heterosexual couples.

In a free society, people do ultimately have the right to go to hell in their own way. Often there is no way to stop them from taking others—especially their own children—along for the ride. But leaders can and must try to champion what is right. They can speak against bigotry where bigotry is tolerated. They can uphold the equality of women where women are denigrated. They can champion life, even when powerful social forces wish to be liberated from ethical constraints. They can speak to the role and importance of family. They can do all that even if the leaders of the government have led flawed personal lives themselves: If only the morally perfect are allowed to defend the family, then the family will go undefended. And they can stand for marriage against attack—for it is during the next Republican presidency that marriage will come under constitutional and legal attack as it has never been attacked before.

As we uphold human dignity against new technologies and new challenges, however, we have to open ourselves too to some uncomfortable questions about our own ideas and our own practices.

Conservatives achieved enormous success against crime in the 1990s by sending more criminals to jail and holding them there longer. By the end of 2006, more than 2 million Americans were serving time in prison. These methods have worked—but at a terrible price.

Prisons do a good job of protecting the law-abiding. They do a very bad job of reforming the criminal. Two-thirds of state prisoners are re-arrested within three years of release. Prisons harden not only the criminal, but his children as well: The children of prisoners are five times as likely to serve time as the children of non-prisoners.

Nobody really has any good idea how to address this problem. The best scholarly verdict on a century of prison rehabilitation schemes is: "Nothing works." Some conservatives make large claims for the prison ministries of evangelists like Charles Colson. These programs do seem to work for those who choose them. But those prisoners who seek out rehabilitation programs have already completed on their own the most important and most difficult part of the job before the first rehabilitation session even begins.

One thing we can say: If we are going to incarcerate nearly 1 American out of every 100—and more than 1 in 10 young black men—we ought at least to insist that American prisons meet the standards of basic decency. If we cannot rehabilitate, we ought at least not to brutalize. As Senator Sam Brownback of Kansas and other Christian conservatives have urged, this obligation falls especially heavily on Republicans, as the party of law and order, the party whose policies send so many offenders to prison in the first place.

One activist group estimates that some 240,000 men are raped in prison every year—as compared to 90,000 male-on-female rapes reported in the whole country.[39] Reduction of prison rape will require (costly) changes in the way prisons are built and operated, but first and foremost, it will require a change of attitude, away from the prevailing "throw away the key" to a recognition that prisoners remain human beings with rights.

The Democrats' top prison reform proposal is the restoration of voting rights to felons. The self-interestedness of this proposal is obvious—and breathtaking. They assume that ex-cons will vote for them (not a boast you would think they would be proud of). And so rather than take the political risk of working to soften prisons, they seek to gain political advantage from the anger and alienation of those whom prison has hardened.

Physical security; opportunities for education and self-improvement; conjugal visits; mentoring and support for prisoners' children; enjoyable food: We conservatives should stop dismissing these as wasteful fripperies. Prison prevents crime, and so conservatives of course support prison. But prison is a harsh and ugly thing. To sustain political support—and moral justification—for today's tough law-and-order regime, we conservatives must accept the obligation to ameliorate that harshness and ugliness to the extent we can.

If ever there were a cause for a compassionate conservatism—if ever those words meant something—prison reform is it. Someday some intrepid researcher in the Bush administration archives may find in some obscure file the memo from me arguing this point (unavailingly as usual). With a few changes of phrasing and a little updating of the statistics, it might offer a useful start to a future president who seeks to infuse justice with gentleness.

SEVEN

GOAL FOUR:
Green Conservatism

What voters say about the environment is not necessarily what voters want.

Ask them, and voters will tell you that the environment hugely matters to them. In 2005, three-quarters of Americans surveyed—and 60 percent of Republicans—told the Harris survey they agreed that the environment must be protected "regardless of cost."[1] A 2006 MIT survey found that more than one-quarter of Americans now describe global warming as a "serious problem."[2] Yet typically only about 3 percent of voters cite the environment as their top concern in post-voting exit polls.

Even self-described environmentalists can seldom remember an election in which a candidate's stand on environmental issues ranked among the two or three most important reasons for their vote.[3]

To understand why this should be so, you have to understand that what voters mean when they talk about "the environment" is very different from what professional environmentalists mean. For voters, the term "the environment" covers a vast array of not very

closely related issues, from local water quality to unwanted development to (often false) beliefs about the health risks from industry and
technology.

The voters who claim to care most about the environment are
not (as some might expect) the wealthiest voters, but the poorest.
Women claim to care more than men; single women more than
married women; minorities more than whites; young voters more
than older voters.[4]

Yet these "environmental voters" are also the most politically
ill-informed. One dramatic survey from the mid-1990s, for example,
found that women were only one-third as likely as men to answer
correctly questions about current events. This "knowledge gap"
gaped just as wide for college-educated women as it did for women
who had dropped out of high school. Younger voters are radically
more ignorant than older voters. Voters over sixty-five give correct
answers four times as often as did voters under age thirty.[5]

For many of these "environmental voters," environmentalism is
a symbol rather than an issue, a set of attitudes rather than a set of
policies. One-third of young voters claim to regard the environment
as the "most important" issue to them. Now ask them which 2008
candidates they feel enthusiastic about. The candidate who generated the most enthusiasm, Barack Obama, has almost no environmental record to speak of, other than his Democratic party-line
votes. The candidate with the strongest environmental record, John
McCain, generated zero enthusiasm among younger voters.[6] Clearly
here, "environmentalism" stands in for something else—a vague
perception that a candidate is modern, caring, and progressive.

The perceptual nature of the environmental issue may clarify
something odd about environmental politics. The record shows that
almost all of the major federal actions to protect the environment
occurred under Republican administrations: the Clean Air and Clean
Water Acts of 1970 and 1972, the Endangered Species Act of 1973, the

1976 hazardous-waste law known as RCRA, the 1990 Clean Air Act that effectively put an end to the acid rain problem. The list of major Democratic accomplishments hardly bears comparison: the Superfund hazardous-waste cleanup of 1980 pretty much exhausts the list. Yet the Democratic Party owns the environment as a political issue. Americans have consistently rated the Democratic Party "more trusted" on environmental issues since the 1970s. You do not have to do good to win environmentalist support. You have to look good, and at that, Democrats have excelled. President Clinton, for example, twice bypassed Congress to designate national monuments: once on the eve of the 1996 election, the second time on the eve of the 2000 election. The photo op from the 2000 designation got especially wide play: Clinton on the lip of the Grand Canyon, announcing a doubling of the size of the Grand Canyon national park. It went unmentioned that the lands he was designating already belonged to the federal government, and that many feared that the designations were more likely to accelerate unwanted development (by promoting tourism over lower-key local economic uses).

George W. Bush never enjoyed Clinton's easy options.

The environmental groups that had kept so quiet during the Clinton years abruptly declared an environmental crisis the moment a Republican took the White House. For eight years, environmental groups accepted that climate change was a long-term issue that required a careful and measured response. Then George W. Bush took office—and suddenly there was not a second to lose, everything had to be finished by next Tuesday.

The Clinton administration had signed the Kyoto treaty on climate change in 1998. Clinton then prudently refrained from submitting the treaty to the Senate for more than two years. That excited almost zero complaint. Bush in April 2001 announced that he too would not send the treaty to the Senate—and a huge storm of controversy instantly broke over his head, both in the United States and in Europe.

Clinton had the benefit of a collapse in world energy prices. In the summer of 1998, you could fill the tank of a midsized car and get change back from $20. Market conditions soon reversed themselves, however. The average family's energy bill rose 25 percent in Bush's first year in office. From an environmental point of view, this increase surely qualified as good news: Higher prices force conservation.

Environmentalist groups understand very well, however, that while higher energy prices promote environmentalist goals, they destroy the environmentalist political constituency. When energy prices rise, voters quickly abandon their environmental concern. In the spring of 2005, after four years of steadily rising prices, 49 percent of Americans told the Pew poll that it was more important to develop new energy sources than to protect the environment. That summer, Hurricane Katrina hit—and the price of gasoline at the pump abruptly jumped by a shocking $1 a gallon. By September 2005, 58 percent of Americans rated development ahead of environmental protection.[7] Almost one-tenth of the American public had reversed its environmental priorities in the space of four months.

Shrewdly, then, environmental groups have always taken care to promise Americans that green energy will be cheap energy. Unfortunately, this claim involves environmentalists in serious untruths: Electricity from wind, for example, costs almost three times as much as electricity from coal. Hybrid cars cost $2,500 to $3,000 more than comparably equipped gasoline vehicles.[8] Even more unfortunately, the falsity of their promises pushes environmentalists toward infantile conspiracy theories. It's an obvious question: If green power really is as cheap as fossil fuels, why aren't we using green power already? The answer must be the sinister power of Big Oil and Big Coal, forcing themselves on the U.S. economy through their occult machinations. Admit, however, that coal power costs about 4 cents a kilowatt-hour and wind power about 12 cents, and you confront a very different story, in which the environmental villain turns out to be . . . the desire of ordinary people for a better life. In this story, environmentalism may be progressive, but it is about as populist as a regatta at the Newport Yacht Club. Embarrassing! And unacceptable! For environmentalists, the price of political popularity seems to be willful stupidity.

This conundrum hit especially hard during the California electricity crisis of the spring and summer of 2001. In the first months after George Bush's inauguration, more than 1 million Californians suffered power outages. The state's biggest utilities teetered toward bankruptcy. Billions of dollars of California state revenues vanished into the greedy maws of predatory energy traders, and in 2003 California Governor Gray Davis imposed heavy new taxes to repay the cost of the debacle.

Who was to blame? California had adopted a bizarre energy deregulation in the 1990s that freed wholesale prices while capping retail prices. The key assumption behind the plan was inspired by the work of the environmentalist economist Amory Lovins, who argued that Americans used energy so wastefully that forcing conservation could actually improve economic performance. By holding retail prices low, the California law removed the incentive to build new plants. By allowing wholesale prices to float, the law threatened utilities with higher costs. In retrospect, the potential for disaster seems obvious, but California legislators persuaded themselves otherwise. They were impressed by the theory Lovins elucidated in, for example, this 1986 interview:

> Utilities invest about $35 billion a year building power plants that they don't need, can't afford, and won't be able to pay for. . . . They need to be rescued, and I think electrical savings do indeed make it possible to pay off abandoned plants and lower the rates at the same time. Utilities can

finance super efficient lights, motors and appliances. People will then need less electricity so the utilities can burn less coal and emit less sulfur, but mainly everyone will save pots of money because efficiency costs less than coal, and some of that saving can be used to clean up the dirty plants and the rest to lower the rates.[9]

A powerful theory, sullied only by one unfortunate contradictory fact: the advent of the microprocessor revolution and the explosion in demand for electricity to fuel personal computing devices and the Internet. Technology guru Peter Huber has calculated that a single personal computer and its peripherals add about 5 percent to the average annual power bill. The offices of Sun Computer consume as much power as a small steel mill.[10]

California voters recalled Davis from office in October 2003, but Davis succeeded in sharing the blame with Bush. More than half of all California voters rated Bush's performance during the energy crisis as "poor" or "very poor." The President's approval ratings in the state, never great, tumbled a dozen points below his approval in the rest of the country. A belated visit to the state in May 2001 only aggravated his unpopularity. His national ratings slumped too: By June, only 25 percent of Americans credited Bush with paying attention to the issues that "mattered most to them."

Everything the President did to respond to these grim economic realities worsened his political problems. Americans wanted cheaper gasoline? Bush proposed to open more of Alaska and the Gulf of Mexico to exploration, only to be accused of serving Big Oil. Americans wanted more reliable electricity? Bush called for building more power-generating capacity, and Europeans and environmentalists condemned him for warming the planet. Global warming a problem? Bush pointed out that nuclear power emitted no greenhouse gases, terrifying women voters, who overwhelmingly disapprove of nuclear.

Bush's Democratic opponents promised that they could square this circle. They promised, in the words of Nancy Pelosi, "an energy policy that will reduce energy prices, reduce our dependence on foreign oil, and reduce pollution."[11]

How would that work?

Reduce energy prices? Lower energy prices encourage consumers to use more energy, emitting more pollution.

Reduce dependence on foreign oil? But we import Saudi, Venezuelan, and Nigerian oil precisely because it is the cheapest fuel available. Any substitute will cost more.

Reduce pollution? Green technologies cost much more than conventional fuels.

Democrats promise that fabulous new alternative-energy technologies await us just around the corner. All it will take is just a very few additional federal dollars to bring these technologies to market. . . . Call this the Tinkerbell approach to policy: Clap your hands and say, "I believe in alternative technologies, I do, I do, I do." But these technologies have been collecting tens of billions of dollars in federal subsidies since the 1970s. Unlike Tinkerbell, they never do quite flutter to competitive life, no matter how fervently their sponsors mumble incantations over them.

With enough federal dollars, you can make alternative fuels look cheap. Give wind producers a big tax credit and they can compete with coal. But tax-subsidized energy is not the same thing as cheap energy.

The beginning of wisdom on the energy issue is to recognize that we can achieve at most two of the things Nancy Pelosi wants, but never all three. We can have clean American power. We can have cheap American power. But we cannot have power that is clean and cheap and American.

To govern is to choose. If we can have only two of the three benefits, Republicans should choose power that is American and clean—but not so cheap. Republicans should do so for the reasons laid down by Adam Smith in *The Wealth of Nations*: "Defense is superior to opulence"—or, in modern English, because national security is worth paying for.

And Republicans should also do so because it is past time for us to rediscover our lost history as the party not only of conservatism but of conservation. We have to be careful here. Conservatives are often advised to adopt environmentalism. The elitist nature of much modern environmentalism renders this advice very dangerous. In the United Kingdom, for example, David Cameron's Conservative Party has called for heavy taxes on air travel. British families would be allowed one low-tax air trip per year. After that, they would have to pay heavy taxes designed to discourage flying for pleasure. And indeed it is true that air travel emits a lot of carbon dioxide. It's also true that there is something off-putting about David Cameron, ex-Eton, ex–Oxford's Bullingdon Club, heir to an old gentry name and fortune, telling his class inferiors to take their vacations at home.

On this side of the water, too, there is no shortage of hypocrisy and class prejudice in the climate-change debate. In 2005, I attended an event at which one entertainment industry stalwart after another announced with pride that they had just replaced their Range Rover or Lincoln Navigator with a hybrid car. Later, a cynical friend who knows Hollywood advised: "You should have asked them, 'Who has your Range Rover now?' If they're honest, they'll tell you—they gave it to the maid. After all, you can't go to Costco or pick up the kids from Crossroads in a Prius. So all over Westside L.A., you saw tiny brown women driving huge Lincoln Navigators."

Hollywood environmental activist Laurie David swaps out the Charmin in her mansions for rough paper made from recycled fibers—but flies by private jet. Al Gore's principal home consumes as much electricity in a month as the average American residence consumes in a year. Gore explains that he is "carbon neutral" because his hedge fund offsets his emissions by using other people's money to make virtuous energy investments on his behalf. (It's a very bitter irony indeed that it is George W. Bush who built his ranch as an environmental showplace, down to the recycling of rainwater, while Gore did not get around to installing solar panels on his Belle Meade mansion until six years after he moved in.) These examples of environmentalist hypocrisy reinforce the image of liberals and Democrats as arrogant and out of touch. Why would Republicans allow their Christie Todd Whitmans to saddle such an image upon them as well?

Yet it is also true that for all its absurdities, a revolution in environmental consciousness has come to modern societies. Americans will not remain indefinitely immune to the huge political shifts that have remade politics everywhere else in the developed world. As people get richer, material things come to matter less, things of the spirit matter more. Or, as an economist would say, the marginal utility of money declines as you acquire more of it, while leisure, tranquillity, and beauty come into greater demand as people acquire greater ability to pay for them.

America has very genuine energy problems. Heavy consumption of petroleum enriches sinister autocrats, emirs, mullahs, and kleptocrats. And despite the often hysterical exaggerations of the green lobby, pumping trillions of tons of carbon dioxide into the atmosphere cannot be healthy.

As Republicans and conservatives, we have to keep the economic hardships of ordinary families in mind as we address these problems.

The average American family uses over 1,500 gallons of gasoline per year. Even a 50-cent increase in the price of fuel makes a real difference to the average family's budget. By 2007, after seven years of energy price increases, the typical American family was spending about 9 percent of its income on energy, or as much as it spent on clothing and entertainment combined.[12]

These costs bear hardest on our voters, in the middle of the middle class.

Conscience also compels us to bear in mind the hardships of the global poor. Curbing carbon emissions will slow economic growth worldwide. The best estimates suggest that full compliance with Kyoto could cost the planet $150 billion per year. To put that into perspective, that is more than double UNICEF's estimate of the cost of providing clean drinking water and basic sewage service to every inhabitant of the Third World.[13]

Republicans must balance environmental protection against economic development, national power, and middle-class interests. For us, the environment is not a substitute for religion, but a series of interlocking practical problems that must be solved to meet our supreme political priorities: maximizing the power and prosperity of the United States while responsibly enhancing the well-being of American families.

All Americans would of course prefer the cheapest possible energy source. But cheap energy means oil, and not just any oil. Cheap energy means Persian Gulf oil—because the Gulf states are the world's lowest-cost producers. And as we have been painfully reminded over the past half-decade, Persian Gulf oil means trouble.

The world burns 80 million barrels of oil a day. The United States produces only about 7.5 million of those 80 million barrels. Canada and Mexico together produce 7 million more. Norway contributes a little shy of 3 million. Toss in the United Kingdom and Brazil—stretch a point and include Gabon, Indonesia, and Kazakhstan—and still only about one-third of the world's oil comes from countries that can be counted on to behave responsibly.

Now look at the other side of the ledger: Approximately 9 million of the 80 million barrels come from Russia. Another 9 million come from Saudi Arabia. Add 4 million from Iran, 2½ million from Venezuela, and 2 million from Nigeria, the output of the other Gulf states, scattered production elsewhere in Asia and Africa, and all told, almost two-thirds of the world's oil revenues are paid to people likely to put them to bad use. At $50 a barrel, America's oil imports underwrite $1 trillion a year of extremism, corruption, authoritarianism, aggression, terrorism, and general mischief.

The global supply picture for natural gas looks even worse. Half the world's natural gas reserves are located under Russia and Iran. Add Algeria and Qatar, and you have accounted for almost three-quarters.

Between 2002 and 2007, Russian military spending quadrupled.[14] Iran's military spending cannot easily be assessed, but certainly the tempo of the Iranian nuclear program has accelerated as Iran's oil revenues have risen since 2002. Credible sources estimate that Hugo Chavez's Venezuelan government has spent as much as $12 billion to support authoritarian political parties in Central and South America.[15] Saudi missionary—or *da'wa*—spending is also hard to trace, but it is often estimated at $70 billion since 1979: an important cause of the spread of Islamic radicalism worldwide. The Saudis are widely believed to have helped finance the Pakistani nuclear bomb program.

The oil and gas consumption of the advanced Western economies does worse than enrich these bad actors; it empowers them. Natural gas, for example, travels by fixed pipelines. Once the pipeline is built, supplier and customer depend on each other. Since 2002, Russia has abused that power to intimidate its neighbors—and indirectly, Western Europe. The Russians cut Ukraine off entirely in 2006 and Belarus in 2007. The cutoff disrupted gas markets throughout the continent. The Saudis whisper promises to increase oil production (and thus help reduce prices) to avert negative consequences when caught doing things objectionable to the United States, such as, for example, allowing fund-raising on their territory to support the Sunni insurgency in Iraq. The Iranians seem to delight in panicking international oil markets, earning windfalls from their own provocative behavior.

So our first energy priority must be: Lead the world to consume less oil and gas. This may sound like an unrealistic goal. Far from it.

Many people imagine that America's energy use always goes up, up, up—that Americans are helplessly, uncontrollably "addicted to oil," in the words of President Bush. Wrong metaphor. Addicts will pay any price to get their fix. American oil consumers respond to price signals. After the oil shock of 1979, American oil consumption declined by almost 3½ million barrels a day. Not until 1996 did American oil use recover to the levels of the late 1970s. Even by 2005, Americans were using only 17 percent more oil than they did three decades before. Oil consumption in other advanced Western nations followed a similar pattern.

The oil shock of 2003–2005 has likewise altered consumer behavior. Sales of Lincoln Navigators and Ford Expeditions dropped 55 percent between 2004 and 2005. Over the same period, sales of Honda Civics jumped 30 percent. Housing sales in exurban neighborhoods slowed. The National Association of Realtors reported that 9 percent of homebuyers listed "short commute to work" as a prime house-buying consideration in 2005; 40 percent said so in 2006.[16]

But all this conservation comes with a grim ironic twist. High prices encourage consumers to use less. High prices also induce new higher-cost supplies of oil to come to market. (Production from Canada's vast but costly oil sands is projected to double between 2005 and 2010, and then double again between 2010 and 2015.) Increased supply and reduced demand will lead to—anybody? anybody?—yes, that's right, a drop in price. And that restarts the whole cycle. As prices decline, higher-cost oil is driven off the market, consumers begin revving up demands, and a decade later, the oil producers have recovered their power.

We have to break this cycle.

Congressional Democrats and President Bush have shown us how not to break it. Both of them advocate large-scale government intervention in energy markets to subsidize alternative fuels (especially ethanol) and new technologies (hydrogen cells, electric cars, and so on). This is the path the United States took in the 1970s, and it led to very little progress and enormous waste. Indeed, future budget director David Stockman cited the Carter administration's boondoggling synthetic fuels program as the outstanding example of waste in the whole federal budget inherited by Ronald Reagan in 1981. Now it is a Republican president who proposes to repeat the mistake.

Republicans should stand for a radically different approach. We should strenuously oppose government playing investment banker, directing capital to this technology or that one. We should oppose all subsidies, special favors, tax credits, and other market-distorting and wealth-destroying interference.

There is a simpler and better way to encourage consumers to conserve while denying income to producers: Tax those forms of energy that present political and environmental risks—and exempt those that do not. That tax will create an inbuilt price advantage for all the untaxed energy sources, which could then battle for market share on their competitive merits.

What would such a tax look like? It would fall heavily on oil, natural gas, and polluting coal—more lightly on ethanol—and it would exempt hydropower, solar, wind, geothermal, and nuclear altogether. In short: It would look exactly like the carbon tax advocated by global-warming crusaders.

A tax of $50 per ton on carbon emissions would raise the price of a barrel of oil by $6. At current usage levels, such a tax would generate over $120 billion in annual revenue for the U.S. Treasury. If the tax cut oil use back to 1995 levels, it would still generate more than $100 billion—more than enough to fund major tax reforms.

You don't have to believe that global warming is a problem to recognize that a carbon tax is the solution. Under the umbrella of a permanent disadvantage for fossil fuels, markets could figure out freely which substitutes made most sense.

A carbon tax would impose disproportionate costs on the poorest consumers. Solution: Dedicate the first portion of the revenues from the carbon tax to funding the reform in the child tax benefit I discussed in Chapter 5. The additional hundreds of dollars in payroll tax reduction for working-class families would more than offset the burden of the new energy tax.

A carbon tax would finally open the way to the expansion of nuclear power that even Al Gore has reluctantly endorsed. The United States derives 20 percent of its electricity from nuclear power. Japan gets 33 percent; France, 80 percent. Yet the growth of nuclear power has stalled: No new reactor has been ordered in the United States since 1978.

No question, nuclear power presents challenges, with safe storage of nuclear waste heading the list. Teams of engineers have repeatedly identified Yucca Mountain, Nevada, as the ideal storage site in the continental United States—but with a Nevada senator occupying the majority leader's office, it will be difficult to put science ahead of politics. On the other hand, Republicans and conservatives should emphasize and emphasize again that the alternative to nuclear power is not windmills or solar panels or mulch power. The alternative is coal: cancer-causing, climate-changing, miner-killing coal, which generates more than half of all the electricity used in the United States.

Coal mining killed 47 people in 2006 and injured over 5,000 more.[17] The burning of coal for electricity accounts for one-third of all the carbon dioxide emissions of the United States.[18] Perhaps of greatest relevance, the very cheapness of coal discourages energy conservation and the development of energy alternatives.

Energy efficiency is not simply a matter of turning off the lights. Conservation costs money. A new air conditioner may use one-third the power of an older model—but the old one is paid for and the new one must be bought. Consumers and firms will only invest in energy efficiency when those efficiencies make economic sense.

A little history illustrates the point. In 2004, the U.S. economy used less than half as much energy to produce a dollar of wealth as it did in 1949. Progress! But the progress came a lot faster when energy prices were high than when energy prices were low. In the cheap-energy era from 1949 to 1973, the U.S. economy improved its energy efficiency at a rate of only about 0.5 percent per year. In the expensive-energy era from 1973 to 1985, energy efficiency improved at a brisk 2.6 percent per year. After the energy price slump of the mid-1980s, however, efficiency gains slowed again, to 1.6 percent per year.[19]

An improvement of 1.6 percent per year in energy efficiency may look pretty good. But there is reason to fear that this number distorts the energy record. Remember, the 1990s saw a sharp tilt in the U.S. economy away from manufacturing and toward services. Much of what looks like an improvement in energy efficiency really reflects a decline in heavy-energy-using sectors of the economy. Adjust for that reality, and the energy efficiency picture of recent years looks less flattering: The U.S. Department of Energy estimates that what it calls "energy intensity"—efficiency improvements within the same sector of the economy—improved by only 10 percent in the whole two decades from 1985 to 2004.

Your steel industry dies only once. The United States has now largely completed the transition from a heavy industrial economy to a high-technology and service economy. Within those new sectors, it seems that efficiency gains have slumped back down to the 0.5-percent-per-year level of the 1949–1973 period.

A carbon tax would raise the cost of coal-generated power and enhance the competitiveness of alternatives. Of the non-carbon-emitting alternatives, nuclear is both cheapest and most effective.

One modern midsized nuclear reactor—such as the Westinghouse model Duke Power is proposing to serve its growing market in the Carolinas—produces as much electricity as 800 wind turbines, at approximately two-thirds the cost. (And without killing birds.)

A carbon tax would also do more than any other measure to accelerate the shift away from gasoline-powered cars in a rational, cost-effective way.

Which makes most sense: Conversion from gasoline to ethanol? Or to hybrid gasoline-electric cars? To focus on incremental improvements to existing cars to raise their mileage? Or to jump ahead to some entirely new technology as an alternative to the internal combustion engine? The honest answer is that nobody yet knows. For government to decree one solution or another will almost certainly end in waste and disappointment. A higher gasoline price—combined with the abolition of all other subsidies—will clear the way for market competition to settle the issue.

President Bush has often declared that it "makes sense" "to promote ethanol as an alternative to foreign sources of oil."[20] Maybe it does; maybe it does not. Either way, it is not for a politician to decide. Tax oil, raise its cost to consumers, and create an equal opportunity for all oil alternatives to battle it out, with no special advantage for those oil alternatives that use Iowa corn. That is the politicians' responsibility, and it is plenty big enough. Investors and entrepreneurs can finish the job.

Some conservatives and Republicans—including President Bush—want to limit the problem of oil to "foreign oil." The problem, they say, is that America imports "too much": close to 60 percent of America's 20-plus-million-barrels-per-day usage. But this, I'd argue, is a very mistaken way to look at the problem. Oil is a globally traded commodity. There is one world oil market, one world price. The problem of Persian Gulf oil would loom huge for American security even if every pint of America's oil were pumped in the fifty states.

Indeed, even as it is, only about 10 percent of America's total oil consumption comes from the Persian Gulf. The United States imports less oil from Kuwait than it does from the United Kingdom, less from Saudi Arabia than it does from Mexico, and less from anybody than it does from Canada.

But if Iran uses its oil revenues to underwrite a nuclear program, what does it matter whether those revenues are denominated in dollars, euros, or yen?

If Osama bin Laden were to seize control of the Saudi state, would it console us that comparatively little of his oil wealth derived from U.S. sources?

If a regional war in the Middle East disrupted global oil supplies and plunged America's trading partners into economic crisis, would not the New York financial markets plunge just as deep as London or Tokyo?

It is oil consumption, not oil imports, that measures the depths of America's oil dependency.

That's not to deny that it would be a good idea to open more of Alaska and the Gulf of Mexico to oil exploration as a short-term palliative. If U.S. policy could increase the share of the global oil supply that came from reliable producers—the United States, Canada, and others—that would certainly contribute to global stability. But it cannot reasonably be hoped that higher output from reliable suppliers will liberate the world from its dependence on doubtful suppliers anytime soon. We have to recognize that while increased North American oil production will be helpful, only substitution and conservation can achieve the important national security goal of reducing the power of unreliable oil suppliers.

And only substitution and conservation can achieve Republican and conservative environmental goals: practical, moderate, sensible goals that pass rational scrutiny.

Many environmentalists are motivated not by the love of nature but by fierce antipathy to the technological and rational society of the West; not by reverence but by revulsion. They do not seek to preserve. They seek to destroy.

These feelings are obvious in ecological radicals. But they are equally present, surprisingly so, in the minds of some more mainstream environmentalists as well. Listen, for example, to the words of Al Gore from his 1992 book *Earth in the Balance,* perhaps the most artless and unguarded writing ever to issue from the pen of an American politician. Gore believes that Western civilization is founded upon "intense psychic pain."[21] Gore does not want merely to fiddle with the planet's thermostat. He yearns for a moral, cultural, and emotional revolution: "The froth and frenzy of industrial civilization mask our deep loneliness for that communion with the world that can lift our spirits and fill our senses with the richness and immediacy of life itself."[22]

The environmental movement has always trafficked in apocalyptic fantasy. From its onset it has offered one vision after another of impending catastrophe. Sometimes environmentalists warned of a new ice age, sometimes of mass famine provoked by overpopulation, sometimes of the spread of deserts from the equators to the globe, now latterly that carbon dioxide will melt the polar icecaps and send super-tsunamis racing toward Manhattan. The specifics fluctuate with the minutes, but the conviction of certain doom never alters.

Perhaps this is why voters' environmental instincts seldom translate into actual environmental votes: Environmentalists seem positively to crave disaster as a righteous judgment on erring humanity. And here may be the secret clue as to why the environmental issue is ripe for plucking by sensible conservatives. As the Canadian journalist Andrew Coyne wittily puts it:

> The voters have an aversion to fanaticism. They may wish you to do some hard, unpleasant thing for them, but they don't want to see you enjoy it. They want whoever they assign the task to be constantly testing the brake. . . . to do as much as [the public] requires of them, and no more.[23]

Who is more likely to be trusted to produce rational, cost-effective measures against global warming: People who waited to act until the evidence became overwhelming? Or people who have been itching for decades to repeal the Industrial Revolution on any excuse they could find?

It is a plain matter of record that the American environment has steadily and substantially improved over the past three decades. As the market-oriented environmentalist Gregg Easterbrook points out:

- Environmental trends are nearly all positive, with all forms of pollution except greenhouse gases in steady decline in the United States and the European Union.

- In the middle 1970s, only one-third of America's lakes and rivers were safe for fishing and swimming. Today, two-thirds are, and the proportion continues to rise.

- Since 1970, smog has declined by a third, even as the number of cars has nearly doubled and vehicle-miles traveled have increased by 43 percent.

- Acid rain has declined by 67 percent, even though the United States now burns almost twice as much coal annually to produce electric power.

Perhaps the single most dramatic example of environmental improvement: "Rocky Mountain Arsenal, outside Denver, where nerve gas was once made and a location regularly described . . . as 'the most toxic place on earth,' has been a National Wildlife Preserve for ten years: eagles and other biologically delicate species now thrive there."[24]

Our task now is to build on these improvements—not to deny them, and certainly not to lapse into doomsday hysteria because sea levels are rising a couple of inches per century.

The Republican Party at its best has expressed America's self-confidence that American knowledge and competence can deliver a better life to all people.

Our message should be:

We trust free people and free markets to solve our energy and environmental problems.

We are going to break America's dependency on oil, gas, and coal not by regulations, but by a tax that makes renewables and nuclear power more competitive with fossil fuels.

Every dime of that tax increase will be rebated back to the American people in the form of tax reductions to working parents and cuts in taxes on productive investment.

At a time when Democrats and liberals seem to have adopted environmentalism as a substitute religion, Republicans and conservatives are ideally positioned to reclaim it for common sense and the common good.

EIGHT

GOAL FIVE:
Win the War on Terror

"I'm pleased with the progress in Iraq."
—President George W. Bush, September 18, 2004[1]

For three grinding years, President Bush assured Americans that America was making steady progress in Iraq. We kept making more and more progress until we had arrived at the verge of total disaster.

Iraq is the great wreck and failure of this presidency, the great enduring shadow on our party. If Republicans and conservatives are to regain their role as the defenders of the nation—and a credible party of government—we must offer a way forward on Iraq. We cannot stubbornly hold on, insisting that all will be well if only given more time. If we do that, we narrow the political choice before the American people to two: Republican status quo or Democratic unilateral withdrawal. The Democratic course may be strategically disastrous, but it will prove politically irresistible, inflicting severe consequences on the nation and our party.

Who can deny that the Iraq war has been a shambles? Even those of us who supported it—especially those of us who supported it—feel frustration and sadness over the way in which it was run.

Mistakes are made in every war, it is said, and that is true. Rarely, though, have so many and such lethal mistakes been made as in Iraq, and probably never in American history have war leaders so stubbornly refused to correct mistakes when exposed.

Democratic leaders like to call Iraq "George Bush's war," and a majority of the American people have disapproved of Bush's leadership on Iraq since February 2004.[2] But Iraq was not George Bush's war. It was America's war, and all Americans will gain or lose according to whether it ends in success or failure.

We are nowhere near the beginning of that end. We are, as Churchill famously said, only at the end of the beginning.

America went into Iraq with two war aims: (1) to end Saddam Hussein's threat to the peace of the region, and (2) to establish a stable Western-oriented government. Aim 1 worked out. Aim 2— not so much.

Some of us are still prepared to defend President Bush's original decision to overthrow Saddam. I would argue that the war would have come to a happier ending with better decisions in 2002 and 2003, and I think I can prove my case. So what? From the point of view of a voter, there's not a lot of difference between plunging into a war that could never have been won—and bungling a war that could have been.

Under George Bush, Republicans have lost their historical advantage as the party of national security. From 1968 through 2001, the Republican Party consistently enjoyed at least a 10-point lead (and often as much as 20 points) on the poll question "Which party do you trust to do a better job on national security?" After 9/11, the Republican lead on security jumped to 30 points. That lead lasted just long enough to reelect George Bush in 2004. And then it collapsed. Vanished. Not since Barry Goldwater cracked jokes about lobbing missiles into the men's room at the Kremlin has Republican credibility on national defense sunk so low.

Iraq heads the list of Republican security calamities. But the other entries fill a page.

What about that Iranian nuclear bomb program? President Bush said in 2002: "I will not allow the world's most dangerous regimes to acquire the world's deadliest weapons. I will not wait as dangers gather." But that is exactly what he has done.

What's the threat level advisory today? Do you know? Do you care?

How many times a week are you asked to present identification to enter a building? Why? How often has that identification ever been checked against any kind of authorized list or computer database? What exactly was accomplished by the now canceled ban on nail scissors aboard airplanes? What is being accomplished by the current ban on mouthwash?

Quick: Who are we fighting in the "war on terror"? Evildoers? Extremists? Islamofascists? If you are "with us or with the terrorists," as the President said, where is Saudi Arabia? Where is the Palestinian Authority? Where is Pakistan? Where is Russia? Where is Mexico?

How is it that America's enemies have succeeded in convincing half the world—and a considerable number of Americans—that the United States is running some kind of gulag torture chamber in Guantánamo Bay?

These questions and many others like them have gnawed away at Americans' confidence in the Bush administration's security policies—and corroded support for Republicans and conservatives.

Republicans and conservatives might respond: The United States has gone six years without a foreign terrorist attack on American soil. And while Europe has suffered two major terrorist attacks since 9/11—the Madrid railway station bombing of 2004 and the London subway bombing of 2005—these two plots revealed the decline of the terrorists' striking power. The Madrid bombing was far less sophisticated than 9/11, and the London attack was even cruder than Madrid: four youths with bombs in backpacks. And when terrorists have attempted anything large—like the Heathrow liquid explosives of August 2006—their plans have been foiled by effective police work.

Islamic extremists have not succeeded in overthrowing the government of Pakistan or any of the Western-aligned countries of the Middle East, as many feared in 2001 they might do.

The Libyan nuclear program has been shut down. Saudi Arabia and the United Arab Emirates have been cajoled and coerced into stronger action against terrorist financing. The Israeli security fence has effectively constrained Palestinian terror. Syria was compelled to remove its military forces from Lebanon. Al Qaeda–like movements have been suppressed in Somalia and the Philippines. And for all the warnings that the Iraq war would split the Western alliance forever, in fact post-Iraq elections have brought pro-American politicians to power in Germany and France.

Like the old joke about Wagner's music, you could see that the Bush foreign policy has been better than it sounds. Henry Kissinger quips that in the Clinton administration the explanations were always better than the policies, while in the Bush administration it was the other way around.

Kissinger was at least half right. The Bush administration's explanations were terrible. Unfortunately, a lot of the policies left something to be desired, too.

Here's Secretary of Transportation Norman Mineta describing America's new security screening policy to Steve Kroft of *60 Minutes* in December 2001. Kroft asked: "Are you saying, at security screening desks, that a seventy-year-old white woman from Vero Beach, Florida, would receive the same level of scrutiny as a Muslim young man from Jersey City?" Mineta answered: "Basically, I would hope so."

How to devise a good explanation for the administration's determination to keep the doors of the United States open to migrants from the main sources of terrorism? In 2005, migration to the United States from the Middle East reached something close to an all-time record: An estimated 40,000 Middle Easterners were granted admission to the United States as legal permanent residents that year. (An additional 56,000 Middle Easterners already present in the country also received their green cards that year, the highest level in two decades.)[3]

At the same time as it sped up the entry of Middle Easterners, the Bush administration went slow on removing Middle Eastern illegals. In 2002, the Bush administration actually removed 30,000 fewer illegal aliens than the Clinton administration had removed in 1999,[4] almost none of them from Middle Eastern nations.

You might suppose that the Bush administration at least directed careful scrutiny to Middle Eastern migrants. You would suppose wrong. In the year 1990, Representative Barney Frank of Massachusetts passed what might be called "The Extremist Welcome Amendment" to the immigration laws. Frank's amendment forbade the U.S. government to deny visas to aliens who held extremist views. Under the Frank amendment, an Egyptian university student belonging to the Cairo University Death to America Glee Club or the Jihad Boosters could not be denied a visa when he applied to study explosives technology at a U.S. university. If his "beliefs, statements, or associations" would be legal in the United States, then they could not be used to exclude a migrant. In effect, Frank extended the U.S. First Amendment to the whole planet. Very generous. Also very dangerous. Under the Frank amendment, it would have been illegal for the U.S. Department of State to deny a student visa to Muhammad Atta.

So: Did the Bush administration demand the repeal of the Frank amendment after 9/11? Not at all. Once again: Hard to write a good explanation for that one.

Maybe Bush foreign policy was so hard to explain because it was incoherent at its core. On the one hand, the President defined the war on terror as a struggle as epochal as World War II or the Cold War. On the other, he hastened to assure Americans that the terrorists were a tiny, outlandish fringe group condemned by virtually everybody in the Muslim world.

These statements contradicted each other. If the terrorists numbered only an infinitesimal few, if their atrocities were abhorred and repudiated by almost all Muslims, the administration's security policies made no sense. You do not declare a giant planetary struggle against a handful of nutcases and oddballs condemned by virtually everybody. Who would go to war against the Symbionese Liberation Army?

On the other hand, if the terrorists constituted a global threat equal to those of the Nazis and Communists, did that not imply some kind of mass following among Muslims worldwide? Something less than universal condemnation?

In 2001 and 2002, Bush did not need to sort out this puzzle. When Bush told Americans that the Muslim world overwhelmingly condemned the 9/11 attacks, they believed him: As of March 2002, half the nation agreed that only "some" or "just a few" Muslims held anti-American attitudes.[5] The proportion of Americans expressing positive feelings toward Muslims as a group actually rose after the 9/11 attacks, from 45 percent in May 2001 to 59 percent in November 2001.[6] (The most conservative Americans changed their views most sharply: In May 2001, only 35 percent of conservatives expressed a positive view of Muslims; 64 percent held positive views by November.)

It rapidly became apparent, however, that the President had underestimated the threat. Anti-American attitudes did hold wide sway among Muslims worldwide. Surveys conducted by Zogby International in early 2002—a year before the Iraq war—found that only 13 percent of Egyptians and 12 percent of Saudis expressed favorable opinions of the United States.[7]

In 2004, Senator Kerry accused George Bush of squandering the goodwill of the world. But in the Islamic world, there was precious little goodwill to start with. In Pew's 1999 survey of global opinion, Pakistan ranked as the most anti-American country on earth. From Morocco to Indonesia, from Birmingham to Gaza, the 9/11 attacks detonated an explosion of joyous anti-American rage among the world's Muslim peoples.

"I cannot hide my feelings, I cannot restrain my joy." "[T]he most beautiful and precious moments of my life." "We have been prohibited from showing the happiness and joy that we feel, so as not to hurt the Americans' feelings—although in this case, rejoicing is a national and religious obligation." So wrote three prominent Egyptian columnists in the wake of 9/11.[8]

Even some American Muslims condemned the 9/11 attacks only grudgingly and evasively. The executive director of the Muslim American Political Action Committee, Salam al-Marayati, told a radio interviewer on September 11 itself that the attacks were likely committed by Israeli intelligence. The Council on American Islamic Relations condemned the war in Afghanistan in October 2001. Leading U.S. Islamic charities were exposed as conduits for terrorist money. Polls in 2007 found that almost one American Muslim in ten—and one-quarter of American Muslim youth—viewed suicide bombing sympathetically.[9]

Nor was it anything close to accurate to locate the 9/11 terrorists on the outermost fringe of Islamic thought. Perhaps the most influential cleric in Sunni Islam, Yusuf al-Qaradawi, had long championed suicide terrorism against Israeli civilians. And though Qaradawi did condemn the 9/11 attacks, he condemned with equal vigor any American response against Afghanistan and any Arab government that offered any aid to the United States against bin Laden: "A

Muslim is forbidden from entering into an alliance with a non-Muslim against another Muslim. . . . It is also forbidden to hand over Muslims to others." Qaradawi urged a jihad against any American forces to enter Afghanistan, just as was waged "during the Russian occupation of Afghanistan."[10]

In polls conducted after the July 7, 2005, terror attacks on the London subway, Britons learned that about one in twelve of their Muslim fellow citizens approved of terrorist attacks within Britain.[11] More than one-third of British Muslims, 37 percent, regard terrorist attacks against British Jews as justified. A large minority of British Muslims, about one-quarter, express "sympathy" or "understanding" for the 7/7 bombings.[12] An estimated 3,000 British-passport holders are believed to have undergone terrorist training in Afghanistan or Pakistan. Eighty percent of British Muslims say they feel more Muslim than British.

Opinion surveys suggest that about one-tenth of Europe's Muslim population sympathizes with al Qaeda–type terrorist groups.[13] Anti-Israel terror engages the sympathies of many more. In the Middle East, even higher proportions express support for terrorism against Western countries, and actual majorities support terrorism against Israel and U.S. forces in Iraq.[14] Anti-Indian terrorism enjoys broad support in Pakistan, so much so that President Musharraf has felt obliged to conceal security cooperation with India as a shameful secret.

You can only deny the undeniable for so long before forfeiting your credibility. After years of politicians denying that Islam *has* a problem, a majority of the American public decided that Islam *is* the problem. Between 2002 and 2006, the proportion of Americans who blamed the religion of Islam for encouraging violence and terrorism more than doubled, from 14 percent to 33 percent. An absolute majority of Americans, 58 percent, had come to believe that Islam encouraged more violence and extremism than other religions did.[15]

By a 3-to-1 margin, Americans blamed the Danish cartoon controversy not on the insensitivity of Danish cartoonists, but on Muslim
intolerance of divergent opinions.[16]

Yet this negative reaction is as misguided as the early happy talk.
The United States and the Western democracies are not fighting
a billion Muslims. It's silly to talk about what Islam "is." Islam has
been many things, good and bad, in many different times and places.
Our problem is more than big enough: We are fighting a violent
political movement, rooted in the extremist version of Islam propa-
gated by Saudi money, that strongly appeals to second-generation
Muslim immigrants in the West. We had hoped that the liberation
of Iraq would have weakened this violent and extremist movement.
That hope has been tragically disappointed. But that disappointment
does not mean we can turn our backs either on Iraq or on radical
Islam.

Liberals and Democrats keep rerunning Iraq through the Vietnam projector: Either it's a total success or else we have to cry uncle
and withdraw. As Republicans and conservatives, we should say: We
will not accept defeat. We need a strategy of "second best" for Iraq—
a strategy that says that even if we cannot achieve everything we
wanted in Iraq, we can achieve enough to enhance our security and
advance the fight against terrorism.

Iraqi Kurdistan is emerging as a stable, decent, prosperous, and
pro-Western society. A treaty with Iraq's central government can
authorize U.S. bases inside Iraq, from which U.S. forces can strike at
terrorist groups. Al Qaeda's disregard for traditional authority has
alienated the Sunni tribal leadership in western Iraq. The United
States and Iraq have a common interest in bringing Iraqi oil to market. And the more Iran meddles inside Iraq, the more the region's
other Arab governments seek American protection.

The United States can worry less about Iraq's weak central government and instead strike deals with local power-holders: tribal

sheikhs and urban politicians. The United States has till now urged Iraq's Kurds to keep quiet and contain their aspirations: It's time to rethink that policy and accept maximum Kurdish autonomy.

Those may be less than our maximum objectives for Iraq, but they point the way to a better outcome than anything we were going to get by leaving Saddam Hussein in power. Yes, we as Republicans and conservatives have been politically damaged by Iraq. But not as badly damaged as our liberal and Democratic opponents are by their great Achilles' heels. In Iraq, they have reminded all Americans of their readiness to quit a fight when things get tough. They will be just as ready to quit if things get tougher in Afghanistan. And their liberal and Democratic response to the larger war on terror has been hobbled by their bedrock biases: that in any conflict between Western and non-Western peoples, the non-Westerners are probably right, and that all conflicts are ultimately caused by poverty and resolved by redistribution.

Only conservatives and Republicans can overcome the inhibitions of political correctness and build a new strategy based on reality. Democrats and liberals cannot accept that reality. Which means they cannot build a credible alternative. We can—but only if we turn a new page from the failures of the recent past.

This is not the place to outline a new American foreign policy.[17] Here, I want to talk about the intersection between foreign policy and the future of our conservatism and our Republican Party.

In February 2002, President Bush pledged: "The United States of America will not permit the world's most dangerous regimes to threaten us with the world's most destructive weapons." That pledge has not been honored. North Korea has acquired probably half a dozen crude nuclear bombs. Libya is reneging on its promises to destroy its chemical weapons. Bush said, "I will not wait on events as dangers gather." But dangers are gathering—and Bush did wait.

This waiting has exacted a heavy toll on the credibility of the United States and of our party.

Iran's nuclear program has advanced unimpeded. The regime has effectively crushed all internal challenges to its power. Iran funds Hamas and Hezbollah with impunity. The Bush administration talked very tough about the Iranian threat, so tough that it frightened and offended many who ought to be America's friends. At the same time, the administration acted soft—disregarding even the evidence that Iran was arming and training the killers of American soldiers in Iraq.

We Republicans and conservatives need to turn a new page. We must speak in a more conciliatory way and act in a more decisive way.

We should make clear that we as Republicans and conservatives are ready to go the extra mile on negotiation. Direct talks with Iran? Why not? Why not offer to restore diplomatic relations? Iran will probably refuse, but even if they accept, we will have demonstrated that the United States never hastens to war. We want a peaceful resolution. We hope that sanctions can do the job. But we as Republicans and conservatives must also make clear: We are ready to act if talking fails. American voters need to know: Unlike Democrats, Republicans will never allow mullah-ruled Iran to gain nuclear weapons. Whatever it takes to prevent that outcome, we will do. Whatever it takes. That is what we stand for as a party.

Iran is an Islamic extremist state that wants to become a nuclear weapons state. We face a nearly equal danger from Pakistan, a nuclear weapons state that threatens to evolve into an Islamic extremist state. Pakistan has proliferated weapons—to North Korea, to Libya, among others. The former head of the Pakistani nuclear program tried to sell weapons to al Qaeda. If Saudi Arabia and Egypt ever go nuclear, they will do so with Pakistani technology.

The Bush administration's policy toward Pakistan has followed the same dual track as its policy toward Saudi Arabia. On the one hand, the administration has tried (mostly unsuccessfully) to persuade the Saudis to change their ways, quit funding extremism, and cooperate in hunting terrorists. On the other, it has tried (unavailingly) to convince the American public that the Saudis have changed their ways, have quit funding extremism, and are cooperating in hunting terrorists. In both cases, the United States has often seemed to attach much more importance to personal relationships than to objective facts.

These policies have not worked. The monopolization of power by authoritarian rulers deeply and systematically threatens American interests, and we as conservatives and Republicans must recover our voices to say so. The explanation for Islam's turn toward extremism will not be found in seventh-century Arabia. The explanation will be found in our modern times. The transition to modernity has been painful for all peoples. In Europe, the transition begat fascism, communism, and global war. In China, the arrival of modern ideas destroyed an imperial system that had endured for almost 3,000 years, and triggered internal convulsions that may have led to as many as 100 million violent deaths between 1911 and 1989. Who knows if those convulsions have finished even now? Why should Westerners expect Muslim people to do any better in their transition to modernity than the rest of the human race?

The U.S. government—and Western society generally—has very little ability to help Muslims complete their transition. The next Republican president will have enough work to do without also taking on the job of Caliph of All the Faithful, reinterpreter of the Islamic texts. It is not for an American president to determine what Islam is or is not, to propound whether Islam can or cannot adapt itself to freedom, equality, and science. An American president should champion American ideals: freedom, equality, democracy, and progress.

Our European friends face a huge problem integrating their large Muslim populations. Each of them will have to devise their own answer, consistent with their own traditions. It is interesting, to say the least, that France—the European country that does the least to accommodate Islam—has the best-integrated, least radical Muslim population in Europe.

For the United States, it will be a good start to avoid importing this problem in the first place. Stricter immigration laws could have prevented almost every terrorist incident from 1993 on, including 9/11 itself. Five of the nineteen 9/11 hijackers had violated immigration laws at some point or other. Maybe the most conspicuous example is Ziad Jarrah, the man generally believed to have taken the controls of United Flight 93, the plane forced to earth in Pennsylvania. Jarrah had entered the United States illegally at least five times. He had three driver's licenses, two issued in Florida, the third to a false address in Virginia. On the night of September 9, 2001, Jarrah was stopped for driving more than ninety miles an hour in a rural section of I-95. (It's difficult to avoid the suspicion that Jarrah may have been hoping to be caught.) He was pulled over, produced the Virginia license, was issued a ticket for $270, and was sent on his way.

And here we come to the most fundamental dividing line between right and left, Republican and Democrat. John Edwards has called the war on terror a "bumper sticker." Barack Obama's foreign policy speeches give equal attention to terrorism and bird flu. For Democrats and liberals, the greatest threats are always inanimate objects: It is guns that cause crime, microbes that cause international insecurity.

Listen to Vice President Al Gore's January 2000 speech to the UN Security Council—the first time a U.S. vice president ever addressed that supreme world body. Gore's topic: AIDS in Africa. Gore described the disease as an "aggressor." AIDS, Gore told the

Security Council, "is not just a humanitarian crisis. It is a security crisis—because it threatens not just individual citizens, but the very institutions that define and defend the character of a society." In keeping with that redefinition, Gore announced that the next Clinton budget request would "offer specific funding for the U.S. military to work with the armed forces of other nations to combat AIDS."[18] Even after 9/11, President Clinton could offer this assessment to the 2004 Democratic National Convention: "The 21st century is marked by serious security threats, serious economic challenges and serious problems, from AIDS to global warming to the continuing turmoil in the Middle East."[19] Notice that even the Middle Eastern terrorism is described in vague, passive terms, as if terrorism were an accident that happened to human beings, not an action done by them.

Republicans and conservatives do not underrate the seriousness of pandemic disease and environmental protection. But Republicans and conservatives remember that of all dangers, human aggression remains the most fearful. For us, the defense of the nation from violent attack remains the first and supreme duty of government—and a war once begun is not something from which a nation that wishes to remain great can walk away.

Yet this defense will soon become more daunting than at any time since the 1940s. America's most important allies are fading and weakening; its rivals and possible enemies growing and strengthening. Americans face a future in which they will live more and more alone on this planet.

In 1985, the United States, its NATO allies, plus Japan, Australia, and New Zealand produced more than half the world's goods and services. If current trends hold, that same group of countries will probably produce barely more than one-third the world's output in 2025, not even two decades from now. Almost all of that decline will be accounted for by the relative decline of Europe and Japan. In

2025, the United States will produce almost exactly the same share of global output it produced in 1985 or, for that matter, in 1905. But Europe's relative share will drop by half, Japan's by slightly more than half. Not since the collapse of the Soviet Union will great powers have seen their influence shrivel so abruptly. This time, however, there will not even be the excuse of a crisis, just the slow ossification of societies whose organized interests refused to allow necessary reform.

The average German worker already surrenders 29 percent of his or her earnings solely to pay the benefits of today's retirees.[20] As the retiree population grows, that tax burden can only rise. By 2025, more than one-quarter of the populations of Japan and Germany will be over age sixty-five, and one-fifth the population of Great Britain. How will these overtaxed young workers afford to buy homes and start families of their own? As Robert Shapiro, formerly chief economist to the Democratic Leadership Council, warned in 2007, "[U]nless many things change, 15 years from now a typical European or Japanese will live on about half what an average American will earn."[21]

How will European governments pay the cost of national defense? And who will serve? By the year 2025, for example, France will still outnumber Algeria by almost 20 million people, but the number of men of military age will be almost exactly the same in the two countries.

Provoked by the obdurate, abusive, and destructive conduct of the Chirac government in France, the Schroeder government in Germany, and many European media outlets, some Bush officials and some conservative commentators took grim pleasure in predicting the decline of "old Europe." Irritating and shortsighted European governments can be. So can the U.S. government. But of the world's solidly reliable democracies, more than half are located in Europe. The European Union in total today produces more wealth than the United States, nearly half of all the wealth produced by all democratic countries. A world in which Europe is declining is a world in which democracy is declining.

While Europe and Japan falter, China and India roar ahead. China overtook Italy as the world's sixth-biggest economy in 2005. China surpassed France and Britain to gain fourth place in 2006 and is expected to muscle ahead of Germany in 2008. China will likely take second place by 2015. By then, India is expected to rise above all European nations to rank fourth in the world, behind the United States, China, and Japan.

The rise of China and India is lifting tens of millions of human beings out of poverty. Americans, Europeans, and Japanese have gained new consumers and benefited from lower prices. All have prospered together. Unfortunately—and surprisingly—this epoch of economic growth has also been a time of political reversal.

Since 2000, Russia, Venezuela, and South Africa have moved toward one-man or one-party rule. Hopes for democracy in the Middle East have been blighted. Authoritarian governments have consolidated power in Central Asia and Africa. In the 1980s, the failure of the Soviet Union warned dictators they had to choose between their personal power and national wealth. The takeoff of China in the 1990s offered dictators hope that they could have both—and the dictators are profiting from the lesson.

Modern China is the first authoritarian state since the Kaiser's Germany to combine political repression, economic dynamism, and prolonged survival. (By the time of the 2012 Beijing Olympics, China's post-Tiananmen boom will have lasted twice as long as Hitler's Reich.) That's quite a model for a Vladimir Putin or a Hosni Mubarak.

Not only has China inspired authoritarians—it has enriched them. In 1985, China imported hardly any oil at all. Today, China ranks third among oil importers after the U.S. and Japan. India ranks seventh. Chinese and Indian demand has pushed the price of oil above $50 per barrel, and enriched Vladimir Putin, Hugo Chavez, and the kings, emirs, and mullahs of the Persian Gulf. It is Chinese money that pays for Sudan's war in Darfur, and China's Security Council veto that protects Sudan from the consequences.

Wealth buys power. China's military budget is already half as large as that of the entire European Union, and growing fast. It jumped in dollar terms by 14 percent in the single year 2006. In October 2006, a Chinese submarine defeated U.S. sonar operators and surfaced unannounced five miles from the USS *Kitty Hawk,* well within range of a sub-launched anti-ship missile. U.S. experts described the stunt as "alarming." China is trying to build new Pacific region institutions and organizations that exclude the United States, and it is actively wooing authoritarian governments in South America and Africa.

Beyond Iraq, beyond Iran, the next president will have to guide the United States through a world in which America's potential enemies are stronger, its friends weaker, and its values more questioned. Yet there is much that an imaginative and generous Republican president can do to strengthen the nation by aiding its allies.

Over the next decades, the Europeans and Japanese will want to devalue their currencies against the U.S. dollar. A cheaper euro and yen will help create jobs in Europe and Japan and help European and Japanese governments finance their pension obligations. A cheaper euro and yen will also cost jobs in America and reduce the return on U.S. investments in Europe and Japan. For that reason, you would normally expect an American president to resist a euro and yen devaluation. The next president should accept and welcome it.

For decades, Americans have urged the Europeans and Japanese to spend more on their own defense. The next Republican president should accept that it will be very difficult for them to do this. As far and away the richest and youngest member of the Western alliance, the United States will have to shoulder a rising share of the burden.

As the relative power of the Western alliance shrinks, it will become more important than ever for the Western nations to cooperate. The NATO alliance was created to defend Europe against Russia. Under the U.S.-Japan, SEATO, and ANZUS treaties, the United States promises to protect its Pacific allies against China. The United States has the strength to do both, but it does not make the job any easier when European allies sell advanced weapons to China, or when the East Asian allies turn a blind eye to Russian industrial espionage.

We have seen Russia encroaching on the security of its former satellites by practicing energy blackmail on Ukraine and Poland and by waging cyberwar against Estonia. China bullies Taiwan, the Philippines, and Vietnam.

From 1949 to 1991, the North Atlantic Treaty Organization preserved the peace of Europe without firing a shot. Now, like a successful industrial corporation leaping into a new postindustrial era, it is time for NATO to keep its acronym, but drop its name and change its mission from the peace of Europe to the peace of the world.

The next Republican president should press the NATO allies to invite Japan, South Korea, Australia, New Zealand, and Singapore to join—grouping as many willing democracies as possible into a single alliance aimed at countering Russia and containing China.

Pooling dwindling resources, however, will extend Western strength only so far. The Western alliance needs to add new friends. Otto von Bismarck is supposed to have quipped at the end of the nineteenth century that the most important geopolitical fact of the twentieth would be that the United States and Great Britain spoke the same language. So it proved. The United States joined Britain against Germany in two great wars—and the result is that while Britain may have lost her empire, British tourists and businesspeople today need to speak only one language while their German equivalents must learn two.

In the same way, it may turn out to be the most important geopolitical fact of the twenty-first century that the United States shares a language with India, or anyway with the Indian political elite. As America's old allies fade, India with its vast manpower and growing wealth has the potential to assume a grand new role as a U.S. ally and fellow guardian of peace and security in Asia and the Middle East.

Like China, India is an emerging military power, although not yet with anything like China's strength. Unlike China, India is a democracy with a free press and a fair approximation of the rule of law. India and the United States have both been targeted by Islamic terrorism; they both feel apprehensions about the stability of Pakistan; they both have more reason to worry about China than either has to worry about the other.

President Clinton and President Bush both courted India, but Bush worked especially hard, culminating in a 2006 agreement to share nuclear technology. Indian warships patrolled the Straits of Malacca with U.S. vessels in 2001–2002, and conducted large joint exercises in September 2005. India is one of the few countries on earth where the Pew poll finds America becoming more popular. (Although one might well observe—given the traditional anti-Americanism of the Indian elite—that there was nowhere to go but up.)

India will never become as comfortable an ally as the NATO countries have been. Memories of colonialism still sting, and resentment of the West runs strong. India's political stability cannot be taken for granted either, and some of the most vociferously anti-jihadist Indian politicians are motivated by a Hindu chauvinism in many ways as ugly (if less murderous) as the Islamic extremism they oppose. Despite the shared heritage of English-speaking democracy, the U.S.-Indian relationship will be governed more by the cold calculus of self-interest than the warmth of the cultural bond that sustains the Euro-American relationship at its best.

Yet even if the Indians never become intimate partners in the way the Europeans always will be (or as one hopes they always will be), they can at least be strong allies at a time when many European states will have lost their strength. Situated as they are alongside a worrisome Pakistan, outpaced as they probably will continue to be by China, the Indians will want American support and assistance as much as or more than the United States needs theirs. If that ain't love, it'll have to do until the real thing comes along.

To advance this relationship, the next Republican president should take care to stand more closely with India when India next suffers a terrorist attack. Since 9/11, India has been victimized by five major terrorist atrocities:

- A bomb attack on the state legislature in Kashmir on October 1, 2001, which killed 40 people

- A commando attack on the Indian national parliament on December 13, 2001, which killed seven people—but very nearly killed many more, including senior Indian political officials

- Twin car bomb attacks in Bombay on August 26, 2003, that killed 47 and wounded 143

- A series of bombings that killed 59 people and wounded 210 in New Delhi as they prepared for the Hindu festival of Diwali on October 30, 2005

- The Bombay train bombings of July 11, 2006, which killed 174 and wounded nearly 500. As well, suicide bombings and guerrilla violence by Islamic terrorists continue to disrupt life in the state of Kashmir.

The United States has responded to these horrific losses with unattractive coolness. Only once—after the attack on the parliament—did President Bush personally condemn anti-Indian terrorism. The four other attacks, including the Bombay train bombing, merited only a White House press release and a spoken statement by the Secretary of State.

The Bush administration has had pardonable reasons for its dispassion: The government of Pakistan is a crucial, if sometimes duplicitous, ally in the global war on terror. The terror groups that attack India are often based in Pakistan and have in the past drawn support from the Pakistani military and secret services. Moreover, the grievance that inspires these terrorist attacks is the Indo-Pakistani dispute over Kashmir, a dispute in which India's position is not morally strong[22] and in which the United States has not wished to take sides. But Indians do notice the wide disparity in global attention and sympathy received by, say, Spain after the attack on the Madrid train station in 2004 and the sympathy rendered to them. That disparity only reinforces India's always strong sense of national separateness, its nonbelonging to the larger democratic community. This sense of nonbelonging is precisely what the Western alliance must strive to overcome.

If a fraction of the effort wasted upon America's futile public diplomacy in the Arab-speaking Middle East were invested instead in India, the next generation of Americans would reap a very handsome return. For example: While India sent its prime minister of the day to the memorial service at Ground Zero on November 11, 2001, nobody has ever traveled from Washington to attend any of the Indian memorials to its many casualties. The next Republican president should reserve time on his or her first visit to India to meet with families bereaved by international terrorism. And should India ever again suffer an attack on the scale of the 7/11 attack, the next Republican vice president should fly to India to join the national mourning.

The United States should build on the successes of past naval exercises, and invite the Indian army and air forces to join, too. Army doctrine calls on troops to fight as they train. Allied forces that train with U.S. forces fight more effectively alongside them. Forces that train together accustom themselves to the possibility that indeed someday they might fight alongside each other. Senior U.S. officers typically enjoy much closer personal relationships with their Pakistani than their Indian counterparts. But in some crisis fifteen years from now, it may matter enormously that the chief of staff of the Indian army retains fond memories of his year studying in the United States.

Likewise, the next Republican president must resist demagoguery against the phony issue of "outsourcing." Bush economic adviser Greg Mankiw triggered an absurd Washington controversy in 2004 when he suggested that outsourcing represents another form of trade. For stating this indisputable fact, Mankiw was scolded not only by protectionist congressional Democrats but by Republican Speaker of the House Dennis Hastert. To his credit, President Bush addressed the issue directly on his March 2006 visit to India. Speaking to young entrepreneurs at a business college in Hyderabad, Bush said: "We won't fear competition; we welcome competition." And he reminded Americans, "There's a 300-million-person market of middle-class citizens here in India. . . ."[23]

This is exactly right—but something more can be added. The nature of U.S.-Indian trade, with its emphasis on services and direct investment by U.S. companies in India, has the potential to bind the two countries more closely together than does China's emphasis upon manufacturing. A Chinese-manufactured mobile telephone can be sold anywhere on earth; an Indian English-language computer help service has one leading natural market. Indians save only about half as much of their national income as the Chinese do of theirs, which may explain why foreign direct investment in India— and especially U.S. direct investment—is rising so much more rapidly than foreign direct investment in China.[24] India's reliance on

U.S. investment and U.S. customers enhances America's powers of persuasion within India, both economic and geopolitical. The United States has had much greater success since 2000 in dealing with the top irritant in U.S.-Indian economic relations (Indian protectionist regulations) than with the top irritant in U.S.-Chinese trade (China's poor enforcement of patents and copyrights).

Trade must always benefit both parties, or else it would not occur. But some international trading relationships have proven over the years more harmonious than others: There has been much less friction in U.S.-Mexican and U.S.-German trade than in U.S.-Chinese trade and U.S.-Japanese trade. On past experience, the U.S.-Indian relationship gives hope of belonging to the happy first category rather than the troubled second—of becoming a force to draw the two countries closer together politically and strategically as well as economically.

Above all things, however, the next presidency must learn to wage war more effectively than the last.

In Iraq, the United States stumbled into a counterinsurgency campaign without a doctrine or a plan. Unsurprisingly, the campaign was not prosecuted very effectively. The United States has waged and won counterinsurgency wars often in its history: the Philippine rebellion in 1899–1902, battles against communist insurgents in Central America in the 1920s and 1930s, the suppression of the Huk insurgency in the Philippines in the 1950s, the campaign against Cuban-backed guerrillas in Venezuela in the 1960s, El Salvador in the 1980s, and others besides. Where the United States succeeded, it did so by mobilizing local forces with local knowledge. Yet this is precisely what did not happen in Iraq. I'm going to succumb here to the bad Washington habit of quoting oneself:

> Without local allies, we were left to keep order in the cities and villages of Iraq with American soldiers. Our mili-

tary is the best-equipped, best-trained fighting force in the history of the world. But our soldiers are not police: They do not speak the language, they do not know the customs, and they do not know which communal leaders can be trusted and which cannot.[25]

So Richard Perle and I worried in 2003, and these worries have been borne out by events.

One crucial lesson of Iraq—and of Kosovo and Bosnia before it—is that the United States does need to develop some off-the-shelf capacity to "nation-build." We must move beyond the stale and absurd debates of the 1990s in which Republicans only wanted to fight and Democrats only wanted to reconstruct. Fighting is often inevitable, and after it ends, reconstruction is always required. In the 1990s, it was assumed that it would be the job of the United States to fight and of the UN and EU then to rebuild. But the EU of the future will lack the resources, and the UN has proven itself corrupt and incapable. The *Financial Times* has estimated that one-third of all contributions to UN agencies for tsunami relief were consumed by administrative costs. The FT had to rely on estimates, because the agencies involved refused to disclose even basic financial data.[26] Where sunlight has penetrated UN operations, from Oil for Food to African peacekeeping, the light has exposed massive abuse, corruption, and deceit reaching to the UN's very highest levels of leadership.

The United States needs to expand its military police reserve capabilities and build up a U.S. Office of Peacekeeping that can institutionalize the kind of skill and knowledge that the United States scrambled to assemble after the fall of Baghdad. It needs a permanent civilian foreign reconstruction service, rather than relying on military improvisation. It would be useful too to transform the special inspector-general for Iraq into a permanent position that can do instant audits of the honesty and effectiveness of U.S. expenditures in future war zones. The Iraq inspector general, Stuart Bowen, did outstanding work exposing the theft and waste of billions of dollars in Iraq. But he did not start on the job until nine months after the occupation began—and his effectiveness very nearly got his office shut down and himself fired in late 2006.

Probably nobody ever again will try to engage the armed forces of the United States in a tank battle or an aerial dogfight or a ship-to-ship duel. But it would be an equally great mistake to think that all of America's future enemies will rely on guerrilla tactics. Hezbollah's war against Israel in the summer of 2006 revealed the power of missile warfare against even a highly sophisticated military power. As of mid-2006, China has deployed some 800 short-range and medium-range missiles against Taiwan, a force growing at a rate of some 75 missiles per year. China conducted missile "tests" across Taiwan's shipping lanes during Taiwan's first free multiparty presidential elections in the summer of 1996. Hezbollah's success in disabling an Israeli warship with a guided-missile strike in July 2006 and China's surprise surfacing of a submarine within five miles of a U.S. carrier group in November 2006 warns that America's control of the sea will not go uncontested in the future. Russia and Belarus struck a deal in 2005 to deploy new short-range missiles capable of striking former Warsaw Pact nations.

Missile defense, naval supremacy, countermeasures against electromagnetic pulse weapons—all the wizardry that fascinated Donald Rumsfeld remains vital despite Rumsfeld's political fall. It would be the worst and most dangerous error of the Iraq experience if the United States were to draw the lesson that it should abandon military transformation in order to belatedly ready itself to do Iraq over again.

Conventional military power still matters. Naval and air power still matter. Missile defense still matters. The power to defend friends and allies from intimidation still matters. Nuclear superiority matters more than ever. Important as it is to improve America's counterinsurgency capability, it will be positively vital to maintain the power to defend declining friends against rising rivals.

Power, though, is not measured only in ships and planes. America's power has rested as much on its ideas and ideals. In the wake of Iraq, many Americans have turned away from George W. Bush's democracy agenda. An October 2005 survey for the Pew Foundation found that a level of isolationism equal to that seen in 1976, in the immediate aftermath of the Vietnam War. Offered a list of fourteen foreign policy priorities for the United States, "promotion of democracy" ranked dead last.[27]

Yet it remains true: The more democratic the world is, the safer America is. America's worst post-9/11 security challenges can all be traced to actions by supposedly friendly authoritarian regimes in Saudi Arabia, Pakistan, and Egypt. By contrast, even those democracies most vociferously critical of the United States—France, New Zealand, Sweden—discover when the chips are really down that they have much more in common with the United States than divides them from us.

Americans, Europeans, Japanese, Canadians, Australians, Taiwanese, Israelis, and citizens of the other democracies may differ about global warming or the death penalty, about the kind of health care systems they want or the right maximum rate of tax. Yet we all fundamentally agree about the kind of world order we wish to see prevail: a world governed by rules, where individual rights are protected, in which disputes are settled by negotiation rather than force. These are the norms by which we govern our societies domestically, and inevitably our minds regard them as the normal and natural mode to govern the larger society of all mankind.

And indeed this is the way that the democratic portion of mankind *is* governed. When an Italian tourist's Visa card is overcharged by a New York hotel, when a Greek truck damages a Spanish car on a German highway, when a parcel from South Korea goes astray en route to Chile—all involved take absolutely for granted the existence of international mechanisms, public and private, to do equal justice to the citizens of the largest and the smallest nations. And we are all dismayed when these norms are dishonored: when foreign property is stolen, when travelers are imprisoned without cause, when big nations threaten to annihilate the small.

If all this is so, why did the pro-democracy principles repeatedly enunciated by President Bush so miserably fail to resonate with America's allies abroad—and so quickly lose their constituency at home? What insights—and warnings—can the next Republican president take from the disappointments of the Bush years?

The next Republican president's commitment to democratization should be guided by four qualities: clarity, credibility, feasibility, and sustainability.

Clarity first: President Bush never expressed his case for democratization better than in his American Enterprise Institute speech of February 2003: "The world has a clear interest in the spread of democratic values, because stable and free nations do not breed the ideologies of murder." Yet those words raised a question. The ideology of murder that struck the United States had been bred above all in Saudi Arabia, Egypt, and Pakistan. Yet those were the three Muslim countries that the Bush administration showed least interest in democratizing. There were plausible reasons in 2003 for addressing the problems of Iraq before those of Pakistan. Nor is a president required to act like an impartial judge, weighing equally the faults of friends and foes in pristine disregard of the probable consequences of his actions. But it is important that his actions align with his explanations, and the gathering disconnect between President Bush's words and deeds invited the most cynical appraisal of both. The next Republican president should take care to say no more about democracy than he means to do.

Next, credibility: The United States cannot credibly demand that other countries meet international standards of human rights while refusing to acknowledge any such obligation for itself.

There were many opportunities in 2002–2003 for the administration to write—and ask Congress to enact—a legal regime to govern the war on terror. Such laws would have clarified for the whole world the methods the United States intended to use—and those it intended never to use. They would have dispelled the secrecy in which malicious lies grow up and asserted the continuing supremacy of law over the actions of the United States.[28]

Arbitrary power is always terrifying. To reconcile others to American power, that power must be seen to be somehow constrained. If American power is not seen to be constrained by American law, then non-Americans will yearn to see it constrained by some force outside the United States, maybe some force inimical to the United States.

Too often, it seemed that the Bush administration was willing to sacrifice American prestige around the world for the sake of vindicating its legal theories about the scope of executive power. The next Republican president should concern himself less with constitutional theory and more with the need for international and domestic legitimacy.

Third comes the problem of feasibility. Supporters of President Bush often found themselves minimizing the extreme inhospitality to democracy of the culture of the Arab and Muslim Middle East.

Denial of the obvious makes the deniers seem blind, reckless, dangerously naïve. It taints all their true and accurate insights about the connection between tyranny and terror. It transforms them in the public perception from idealists to fools, leading to the absurd result that those who urge the United States to trust Iran, Syria, Hamas, and Hezbollah can get away with calling themselves "realists."

To rehabilitate the democratic idea in American foreign policy, the next Republican president will have to show himself more aware of the difficulties and dangers in its way, especially in the Arab and Islamic Middle East. To make the job seem too easy is to invite Americans to give up on the job altogether.

The fourth and last quality to expect from a new Republican democracy policy: sustainability. American voters and America's friends around the world have come to see "democratization" as a euphemism for ceaseless war: Afghanistan, Iraq, who knows what next—Iran, Syria, Somalia.

This perception is backward. The Bush administration did not overthrow Saddam Hussein in order to bring democracy to Iraq; rather, having overthrown Saddam for classic national security reasons, it then had to leave behind a government in his place—and what other kind of government could the United States bring to power than a democratic one?

More normally, democratization will be a policy in which military force plays only a very subordinate role. When Ronald Reagan told the British parliament in 1983 that he intended to consign communism to the "ash-heap of history," he was not declaring war. He was calling on the nations of the West to advance their values through peaceful advocacy.

> The objective I propose is quite simple to state: to foster the infrastructure of democracy, the system of a free press, unions, political parties, universities, which allows a people to choose their own way to develop their own culture, to reconcile their own differences through peaceful means. . . . It is time that we committed ourselves as a nation—in both the public and private sectors—to assisting democratic development.

This is a challenge that the American people and the peoples of the other democracies can and will sustain.

NINE

GOAL SIX:
Rediscover Conservative Ideals

William Buckley tells of a dinner at the Nixon White House, at which President Nixon pointed out another diner and whispered to Buckley, "Is he one of us?"

Confidential whispering is an old presidential trick, but Nixon's whisper had a special meaning for conservatives. One of us! There had been so few of us in the 1950s, 1960s, and 1970s. The fights were so hard, and we lost so very much of the time. The people in those fights came naturally to look on one another as something much, much more than political allies. They were members of a movement, a remnant, contending against hopeless odds.

One of us! If a conservative heard that somebody had been with Goldwater in 1964 or Ronald Reagan in 1976, why, that conservative had to believe in him or her. They were the veterans of our Brooklyn Heights, of our Trenton, of our Valley Forge. One of us!

Then we began to win elections and change politics, not just in the United States, but all over the English-speaking world. Our numbers grew. But still there was the secret handshake, the freemasonry of shared belief. The numbers grew faster. Political networks ramified, broadened, deepened. New magazines sprang up, new radio celebrities, keeping conservatives in contact with one another, spreading the word. But who decided what "the word" was? Government is so complex, the number of issues nearly infinite. When in doubt, we would turn to . . . one of us.

Some of us began to become very rich. But that was okay. Conservatives had no objection to success. We had achieved a majority in Congress, and business and industry needed representation before Congress. Political success created a positive cycle: Winning elections enhanced conservative political power, and conservative political power opened enticing economic incentives for individual conservatives. They joined lobbying firms, signed up with trade associations, advised corporations and foreign governments. But those were just their jobs. In their hearts, they remained the same as they had always been, didn't they? After all, they were . . . one of us.

At a party near Capitol Hill in the middle 1990s, soon after I had settled in Washington, I listened to a group of congressional staffers and journalists chuckle over a trip they had just taken together to the island of Saipan. They had flown first class, toured some factories, and then spent the rest of their time playing golf or at the beach—all at no cost to them.

Why would anyone spend money to haul a planeload of Republicans to the South Pacific? The partygoers explained that as a U.S. commonwealth, the Mariana Islands to which Saipan belonged were exempt from U.S. immigration and labor laws. The local factory-owners wanted to keep it that way. They had invited these conservative opinion leaders to help them press their case.

I had just caught my first glimpse of the Jack Abramoff lobbying and publicity machine. This was the way the game had always been played, of course, but never had it been played with such big piles of chips. By 2006, some $7 million a day was being spent on lobbying the federal government, most of it in the greater Washington area.[1] Not all of this money ended up in the hands of conservatives and Republicans. But the larger part did.

The trick was to rummage through the inventory of standard conservative beliefs—national security, free markets, local control, freedom of religion—until you fingered one that aligned with the interests of your current client. Then you approached the conservative press, the activist groups, the radio talk-show hosts. You invoked old comradeship, appealed to shared ideals, bought lunch, wrote op-eds—and pushed your hired issue onto the grand conservative agenda. Conservative Washington came to feel like a vast policy Tupperware party, in which people you thought of as friends were continually trying to sell you something.

AT&T, Stolichnaya vodka, local distributors of beer and wine, broadcasters—all hired advocates from the ranks of the Gingrich revolutionaries; all suddenly found their causes receiving a respectful conservative hearing. Conservatism, which began as dissent, then matured into a governing coalition, had evolved into an industry.

At first, this seemed a harmless enough development. From a conservative point of view, AT&T and Stoli were very much in the right in their respective disputes. These were exactly the kinds of fights conservatives had joined in the past for free. Why not make a living at it?

But things quickly got more complicated than that. Effective lobbyists need access and influence. Lobbyists seek favors, and people who seek favors must do favors. A conservative activist tries to persuade politicians to do things conservatives want. A conservative lobbyist often finds himself trying to persuade conservatives to do things politicians want—in return for those politicians doing things his clients want.

This is not a hypothetical or theoretical scenario. In October 2006, President Bush nominated his White House counsel, Harriet Miers, to the Supreme Court. Many conservatives (me included) rebelled against the choice. To manage the nomination through the Senate, the White House called upon super-lobbyist Ed Gillespie. In the 1990s, Gillespie had worked as an aide to House Majority Leader Dick Armey and had helped defeat the Clinton health plan. Gillespie was liked, respected, and trusted in the conservative world. In 2000, he had founded a lobbying firm that billed more than $27 million in its first twenty-four months. It surely did not hurt business to accept assignments from Karl Rove—or to occupy a temporary office in the West Wing. And from that office, Gillespie wagered the reputation he had accrued in the 1990s to push Miers through.

In advance of the announcement of the nomination, presidential adviser Karl Rove placed a call to James Dobson, the very influential social conservative radio broadcaster. Dobson described that conversation on his radio program on October 11, 2005:

> What did Karl Rove say to me . . . ? Well, it's what we all know now, that Harriet Miers is an Evangelical Christian, that she is from a very conservative church, which is almost universally pro-life, that she had taken on the American Bar Association on the issue of abortion and fought for a policy that would not be supportive of abortion, that she had been a member of the Texas Right to Life. In other words, there is a characterization of her that was given to me before the President had actually made this decision.[2]

The dogged *Wall Street Journal* columnist John Fund soon discovered further details of the White House persuasion process.

> On Oct. 3 [2005], the day the Miers nomination was announced, Mr. Dobson and other religious conservatives held a conference call to discuss the nomination. One of the peo-

ple on the call took extensive notes, which I have obtained. According to the notes, two of Ms. Miers' close friends—both sitting judges—said during the call that she would vote to overturn *Roe* [*v. Wade*].

The call was moderated by the Rev. Donald Wildmon of the American Family Association. Participating were 13 members of the executive committee of the Arlington Group, an umbrella alliance of 60 religious conservative groups, including Gary Bauer of American Values, Richard Land of the Southern Baptist Convention, Tony Perkins of the Family Research Council, Paul Weyrich of the Free Congress Foundation and the Rev. Bill Owens, a black minister. Also on the call were Justice Nathan Hecht of the Texas Supreme Court and Judge Ed Kinkeade, a Dallas-based federal trial judge.

Mr. Dobson says he spoke with Mr. Rove on Sunday, Oct. 2, the day before President Bush publicly announced the nomination. Mr. Rove assured Mr. Dobson that Ms. Miers was an evangelical Christian and a strict constructionist, and said that Justice Hecht, a longtime friend of Ms. Miers who had helped her join an evangelical church in 1979, could provide background on her. Later that day, a personal friend of Mr. Dobson's in Texas called him and suggested he speak with Judge Kinkeade, who has been a friend of Ms. Miers' for decades.

Mr. Dobson says he was surprised the next day to learn that Justice Hecht and Judge Kinkeade were joining the Arlington Group call. He was asked to introduce the two of them, which he considered awkward given that he had never spoken with Justice Hecht and only once to Judge Kinkeade. According to the notes of the call, Mr. Dobson introduced them by saying, "Karl Rove suggested that we talk with these gentlemen because they can confirm specific reasons why Harriet Miers might be a better candidate than some of us think."

What followed, according to the notes, was a free-wheeling discussion about many topics, including same-sex marriage. Justice Hecht said he had never discussed that issue with Ms. Miers. Then an unidentified voice asked the two men, "Based on your personal knowledge of her, if she had the opportunity, do you believe she would vote to overturn Roe v. Wade?"

"Absolutely," said Judge Kinkeade.

"I agree with that," said Justice Hecht. "I concur."[3]

Evidence rapidly surfaced to contradict these bold ideological claims. On October 26, 2005, the *Washington Post* published quotations from a speech Miers had given in 1993 strongly suggesting that Judges Hecht and Kinkeade had not accurately represented the nominee's views:

> "The ongoing debate continues surrounding the attempt to once again criminalize abortions or to once and for all guarantee the freedom of the individual women's [*sic*] right to decide for herself whether she will have an abortion," Miers said [in the 1993 speech].
>
> Those seeking to resolve such disputes would do well to remember that "we gave up" a long time ago on "legislating religion or morality," she said. And "when science cannot determine the facts and decisions vary based upon religious belief, then government should not act."[4]

Support for the Miers nomination quickly collapsed, and on October 27, the nominee withdrew.

The President nominated Samuel Alito to replace Miers. Conservatives delightedly supported him, and for a short time it seemed that the breach of trust had been repaired. But as President Bush himself has said: "There's an old saying . . . fool me once, shame on you. You can fool me, but you can't get fooled again."[5]

Conservatives came away from the Miers fight with an uneasy feeling that the president they had elected had tried to take advantage of them. A White House they trusted had tried to deceive them. People they regarded as "one of us" had tried to manipulate them. Not a very nice feeling.

That not-nice feeling kept recurring.

In the Miers battle, the President's team had demanded that their supporters defer to the President's judgment. As one of Miers' strongest radio supporters, Hugh Hewitt, put it in his widely read blog: "The debate ought rather to be an occasion for asking 'What does the president know that I do not know?' and even, 'Has the president earned my trust in this area?'"[6]

When deference failed, Miers' supporters resorted to denigrating the importance of intellect to a justice of the Supreme Court.

"The GOP is not the party which idolizes Ivy League acceptability as the criterion of intellectual and mental fitness. Nor does the Supreme Court ideally consist of the nine greatest legal scholars of an era."[7] So wrote one blogger, phrasing a common line of argument only a little more bluntly than usual. (During the battle, I personally received dozens of e-mails that urged exactly this point, often very angrily.)

Our conservative movement had begun as an intellectual movement. Struggling against the overwhelmingly dominant liberalism of the 1950s and 1960s, conservatives won by out-researching, out-thinking, out-arguing, and out-smarting their opponents. Conservatives in the world of ideas were like U.S. Special Forces: What they lacked in mass and numbers, they more than compensated for with firepower and élan.

Good-bye to all that. In order to support a president's self-indulgent determination to reward a friend, leading conservatives began to argue that intellect no longer mattered to conservative politics.

Marvin Olasky, a former adviser to Governor Bush and the writer who popularized the term "compassionate conservatism," urged all conservatives to emulate the President, and value thinking less and feeling more.

> In so many ways this appointment is classic Bush. Nearly six years ago, when asked in an early debate among Republican presidential candidates to name his favorite philosopher, W famously said, "Christ, because he changed my heart." The pooh-poohing of his answer then (favorite philosopher—the question was about mind, not heart) anticipated the current debate among conservatives: Suffering servant? Why not intellectual leader? It's George W. Bush's analysis that "heart" is crucial, since a good mind by itself also does not a great justice make. He has not only nominated a justice but implicitly called for a paradigm shift in conservative thinking.[8]

The Miers nomination failed, of course. Otherwise, though, Olasky got his wish: More feeling, less thinking had become a new paradigm—if not for all conservatives, then for the Bush administration.

Here was the President's first response to criticism of the Dubai Ports deal in February 2006. Aboard Air Force One on February 21, 2006, the President said of the deal's critics, "One of my concerns, however, is mixed messages. And the message is, it's okay for a Great British company, but a Middle Eastern company—maybe we ought not to deal the same way. It's a mixed message." White House allies pressed the point even more vigorously. "The only whiners left by next week will be the registered bigots," White House ally Grover Norquist told the *Los Angeles Times*.

Ironically enough, this time the White House had the better of the case. The Dubai deal posed no threat to U.S. national security. It had met every legal requirement. The fuss had been whomped up by a U.S. company that feared its particular interests would be damaged. Rejection of the deal made nonsense of U.S. pressure on other countries to open their markets to international investment. But rather than present these compelling arguments, the White House demanded deference. Rather than refute falsehoods, it hurled insults. The Republican Congress did not appreciate this high-handed treatment any better than the conservative rank-and-file had liked it in the Miers battle. Three weeks after Norquist's prediction, the deal lay dead.

Yet the White House did not learn its lesson. The administration and its congressional allies reverted to the same futile tactics of vilification to push its immigration proposals in the summer of 2007. This time it was South Carolina Senator Lindsey Graham who condemned his opponents as "bigots" who should "shut up." The President contented himself with accusing his conservative opponents of not wanting to do what was right for America. Meanwhile, what few actual reasoned arguments the administration deployed were repeatedly exposed as falsehoods. Who could believe that an administration that had failed for almost a decade to complete a visa tracking system required by law would complete a workplace inspection system within eighteen months? President Bush had thrown his pen down in disgust when he signed in October 2006 the bill requiring construction of a border fence. He had failed even to begin design work when the Senate produced its new grand compromise in May 2007. Now he claimed that enforcement would commence just as soon as Congress passed the amnesty he wanted. Again: Who could believe that?

It seemed that the administration's modes of communication had dwindled to three: command, manipulation, and insult. Reason, argument, persuasion: all forgotten.

After Hurricane Katrina, the President spoke to the nation from Jackson Square in New Orleans:

> As all of us saw on television, there is also some deep, persistent poverty in this region as well. And that poverty has roots in a history of racial discrimination, which cut off generations from the opportunity of America. We have a duty to confront this poverty with bold action.

Strong words, but they meant nothing. They did not connect to any serious administration program or plan of action. If anything, administration policy pointed in exactly the opposite direction: In September 2005, the Department of Homeland Security announced that it would not punish Gulf-area contractors who failed to check the immigration status of their workers. Instead of the new war on poverty about which Bush administration staff had mused on background in 2005, the actual result of administration policy was to displace and replace the New Orleans poor. Between 2004 and the end of 2006, the total population of Orleans and Jefferson Parishes dropped by more than 150,000 people. The Latino population, however, jumped from 10,000 to 60,000, as immigrants (many of them illegal) rushed to take reconstruction work.[9] Those New Orleans residents who had been "cut off from the opportunity of America" by racial discrimination now found themselves cut off from the opportunity to reconstruct their own city by the policies of an administration that avowed a determination to help them.

Conservatism, a politics of ideas, a politics once grounded in careful study of the way the world works, had been reduced to grand slogans, to pretty words divorced from reality.

My generation turned away from liberalism because of the collapse of liberal governance during the crisis of the 1970s. We were drawn to conservatism because of the force and allure of conservative ideas. Milton Friedman offered better answers on inflation than James Tobin. George Stigler described the modern economy better than John Kenneth Galbraith. James Q. Wilson's ideas controlled crime better than those of the Kerner Commission. Richard Pipes explained Soviet behavior better than Jerry Hough. Thomas Sowell offered a better route to racial reconciliation than Jesse Jackson. William Buckley outwitted and out-argued Arthur Schlesinger Jr.

Where are the Friedmans now? Where are the Buckleys?

We conservatives have neglected the ideas business for too long. A new generation hungers for answers and solutions, and too often they hear only polemics, wisecracks, accusations, and talking points. The smashmouth conservatism often heard on radio and television can sometimes be good fun, but it does not change minds. It does not even seek to change minds. Smart and funny voices can be heard on the conservative airwaves and in the blogosphere. They daily prove that evidence, patience, and humor can win converts, not just arguments. But tabloid media beget tabloid politics. When you argue stupid, you campaign stupid. When you campaign stupid, you win stupid. And when you win stupid, you govern stupid.

We conservatives have become very good at producing activists and organizers. But intellectually, we are (as they say in retail industry) selling out of inventory. How do we inspire the next generation of activists and organizers? 9/11 has given us a great cause—but the uncertain legacy of the Bush years bequeaths us a very weak case.

Happily for us, our liberal opponents continue to show scant interest in facts and ideas. One influential Democratic writer, the cognitive scientist George Lakoff, gleefully urges his party to discard logic, consistency, and even truth to advance its cause. "To be accepted, the truth must fit people's frames. If the facts do not fit a frame, the frame stays and the facts bounce off."[10] Lakoff then proceeds to propose a series of "frames" that he hopes will rubberize Democratic politicians enough to send even the most inconvenient facts bouncing away. Others, like the psychology professor Drew Westen, urge Democrats to disregard reason altogether, and to rely instead on emotion and confrontation.[11] Even former Vice President Al Gore, in his jeremiad against "the assault on reason" perpetrated by all who disagree with him, himself exposes a strong inward conviction that exaggeration, distortion, and demagoguery offer the surest routes to political success.

But as Ronald Reagan liked to say, quoting John Adams, "Facts are stubborn things." A politics based on "framing"—on words rather than actions and policies—leads only to disappointment and disaster, as we Republicans have had occasion ourselves to learn. Successful politics delivers results, and as Bill Clinton and Robert Rubin proved, modern liberalism delivers results only when and to the extent that it borrows from conservatism. The big ideas of today's progressives—trade protectionism, state-run social welfare programs, a foreign policy that treats the UN as the font of international legitimacy, and central economic planning in the name of energy conservation and environmentalism—will not work any better than they did the last time they were tried. We conservatives and Republicans have at least this advantage in our favor.

This advantage alone is not, however, enough at a time when Americans must prepare to face the decline of their traditional allies and the rise of an aggressive and amoral China; when jihadist terrorists plot murder on a nuclear scale; when the middle class feels itself more anxious and squeezed than at any time since the Carter administration; when new technologies challenge our humanity itself.

It depresses me how many of the smartest young people in politics gravitate to the left. Their politics may be destructive, their ideas knuckleheaded, but they are animated by an enthusiasm and commitment we conservatives too often lack. They remind me of the way we conservatives once were. We must be that way again.

All of us, unless cut off early, end by living in an alien world. I was born in 1960. I am now only a little more than halfway through my actuarially expected life span, and yet I have already outlasted New Deal liberalism, Soviet communism, the Age of Aquarius, U.S. Steel, and a French republic. One of the founding intellectual fathers of modern conservatism, Russell Kirk, used often to invoke "the permanent things." How few of those there really are! The fact of change is the great fact of human life. The accelerating pace of change is the defining feature of modern life. The necessity of adapting to change was the impulse that inspired me to begin this book. And the dangers that threaten any institution or party or political idea that fails to adapt—those were the nightmares that drove me to finish.

ENDNOTES

One George W. Bush: What Went Wrong?

1   Fred Barnes, "Realignment: Now More Than Ever," *The Weekly Standard,* Nov. 22, 2004. http://www.weeklystandard.com/Content/Protected/Articles/000/000/004/916rinyg.asp.

2   Democratic Leadership Council Forum, Nov. 9, 2004. Transcript © *The Congressional Quarterly.*

3   In 1998 and 2000, ethics and morality were the *only* issue cluster on which Republicans polled higher than Democrats: On preserving traditional family values, Republicans led by 16 points; on high ethical standards generally, Republicans led by 17 points.

4   Timothy Noah, "*Slate* Votes," Oct. 26, 2004. http://www.slate.com/id/2108714/.

Two Why We're Losing

1   J. Scott Moody and Scott A. Hodge, "The Growing Class of Americans Who Pay No Federal Income Taxes," Tax Foundation Fiscal Facts (April 14, 2004). http://www.taxfoundation.org/news/show/206.html.

2   Robert Blendon et al., "Understanding the American Public's Health Priorities: A 2006 Perspective," *Health Affairs,* Oct. 17, 2006. http://content.healthaffairs.org/cgi/content/abstract/hlthaff.25.w508.

3   Steve Camarota, "Immigrants at Mid-Decade," Center for Immigra-
    tion Studies, Dec. 2005. http://www.cis.org/articles/2005/back1405.
    html.

4   American Religious Identification Survey 2001. http://www.gc.cuny.
    edu/faculty/research_briefs/aris/key_findings.htm.

5   Jay P. Greene, "High School Graduation Rates in the United States."
    http://www.manhattan-institute.org/html/cr_baeo.htm.

6   Phillip Longman, "The Liberal Baby Bust." http://www.newamerica.
    net/index.cfm?pg=article&DocID=2945.

7   NBC News/*Wall Street Journal* poll conducted by the polling organi-
    zations of Peter Hart and Bill McInturff, Oct. 8–10, 2005. http://www.
    pollingreport.com/budget.htm.

8   Associated Press-Ipsos poll conducted by Ipsos-Public Affairs, Nov.
    3–5, 2004. http://www.pollingreport.com/budget.htm.

9   Gallup poll, April 10–13, 2006. http://www.pollingreport.com/
    budget.htm.

10 Kaiser Family Foundation, *Health Poll Report,* April 2005. http://www.
    kff.org/healthpollreport/apr_2005/1.cfm.

11 Ibid.

12 All data gathered by my AEI colleague Frederick M. Hess, "No Child
    Left Behind: What the Public Thinks," American Enterprise Institute,
    February 1, 2007. http://www.aei.org/publications/pubID.25667.filter.
    all/pub_detail.asp.

13 Pew Research Center for the People and the Press, "Diminished Pub-
    lic Appetite for Military Force," Sept. 6, 2006. http://people-press.
    org/reports/display.php3?ReportID=288.

14 *Newsweek* poll conducted by Princeton Survey Research Associates
    International, Aug. 24–25, 2006. http://www.pollingreport.com/
    science.htm.

15 Gallup poll, March 9, 2001. http://people-press.org/commentary/
    display.php3?AnalysisID=1.

Three How We Win

1   James Bennett, "White House Memo," *New York Times,* Nov. 24, 1997,
    p. A20.

2   Karlyn Bowman, "Polls on Patriotism and Military Service," *AEI
    Studies in Public Opinion,* June 30, 2006. http://www.aei.org/docLib/
    20050630_PATRIOTISM0630.pdf.

3   Hamilton College Patriotism Poll, March 20, 2003. https://my. hamilton.edu/Levitt/surveys/patriotism/.

4   The Pew Research Center for the People and the Press, "The 2004 Political Landscape," Part 3. http://people-press.org/reports/display. php3?PageID=752; "Trends in Political Values and Core Attitudes 1987–2007." http://pewresearch.org/pubs/434/trends-in-political-values-and-core-attitudes-1987-2007.

5   David Brooks, "A Return to National Greatness," *The Weekly Standard,* March 3, 1997, p. 16.

6   In the 2005 Supreme Court case *Roper v. Simmons,* Justice Anthony Kennedy ruled for the majority that the death penalty could no longer be applied to under-eighteens, in part because it violated the UN Convention on the Rights of the Child—a treaty, Kennedy disapprovingly noted, ratified by every country on earth except the United States and Somalia. In dissent, Justice Antonin Scalia scathingly replied: "Unless the Court has added to its arsenal the power to join and ratify treaties on behalf of the United States, I cannot see how this evidence favors, rather than refutes, its position. That the Senate and the President—those actors our Constitution empowers to enter into treaties . . . have declined to join and ratify treaties prohibiting execution of under-eighteen offenders can only suggest that our country has either not reached a national consensus on the question, or has reached a consensus contrary to what the Court announces."

7   Peter Beinart, *The Good Fight* (HarperCollins, 2006), p. 187.

8   Cited in Anand Menon, Jonathan Lipkin, "European Attitudes Toward Transatlantic Relations, 2000–2003: An Analytical Survey" (Groupement d'Etudes et des Recherches, May 2003), p. 8. http:// www.notre-europe.asso.fr/IMG/pdf/Etud26-en.pdf.

9   The federal government only began collecting statistics on volunteering in 2002, and because these numbers rely heavily on self-reporting, most experts doubt their value.

Four   Goal One: A Better Deal for the Middle Class

1   Except for the short-lived Medicare catastrophic coverage program enacted in 1988 and repealed in 1989.

2   Nancy Jo Sales, "Click Here for Conspiracy," *Vanity Fair,* September 2006. http://www.vanityfair.com/ontheweb/features/2006/08/loose change200608.

3   Gary Langer, "Poll: Bush Ratings Tepid, Expectations Mixed," ABC-News.com, Jan. 17, 2005. http://abcnews.go.com/Politics/PollVault/story?id=419276.

4   Cruise Lines International Association. http://www.cruising.org/press/sourcebook2006-midyear/profile_cruise_industry.cfm.

5   Department of the Census, http://www.census.gov/hhes/income/4person.html.

6   Federal Reserve Survey of Consumer Finances 2004. http://www.federalreserve.gov/pubs/oss/oss2/2004/bull0206.pdf. For middle-1980s figure, see Federal Reserve Survey of Consumer Finances 1989. http://www.federalreserve.gov/pubs/oss/oss2/89/scf89home.html.

7   Employment Policy Institute, "Average Real Pre-tax Income Levels, 1979–2003, by Income Group (2003 Dollars)." http://www.epi.org/datazone/06/avr_pre-tax_inc.pdf.

8   University of Michigan, "Surveys of Consumers," July 2006, privately provided to author.

9   Total wages did rise by some 15 percent over those six years, but almost all of the wage growth occurred in the upper ranges of the income distribution. The median income of households, as opposed to individuals, did rise slightly between 2000 and 2005.

10   Pew Research Center for the People and the Press, "Once Again the Future Ain't What It Used to Be," May 2, 2006. http://pewresearch.org/pubs/311/once-again-the-future-aint-what-it-used-to-be.

11   The equality centers were: Franklin, Lincoln, St. Charles, and Warren Counties (around St. Louis); Clinton, Platte, Jackson, and Ray Counties (around Kansas City); Boone County around Columbia; and Greene and Christian Counties around Springfield. Missouri Economic Research and Information Center, "Income Inequality in Missouri 2000." http://ded.mo.gov/researchandplanning/pdfs/sa-1102-1.pdf.

12   See Michael Barone, *The Almanac of American Politics 2004* (National Journal Group, 2005), pp. 929–33.

13   James K. Galbraith and Travis Hale, "Within-State Income Inequality and the Presidential Vote 1992–2004: A First Look at the Evidence," University of Texas Inequality Project, Paper 29. http://utip.gov.utexas.edu/papers/utip_29.pdf.

14   Ed Lazere and Angie Rodgers, "Income Inequality in the District of Columbia Is Wider Than in Any Other Major U.S. City," DC Fiscal Policy Institute, July 22, 2004. http://www.dcfpi.org/?p=55.

15 Ibid.

16 Joel Kotkin, "Urban Legend," *Democracy Journal,* Fall 2006, p. 24. http://www.joelkotkin.com/Urban_Affairs/DAJOI2_20-33_Kotkin.pdf.

17 Jay P. Greene, "How Much Are Public School Teachers Paid?" Manhattan Institute, Jan. 2007. http://www.manhattan-institute.org/html/cr_50.htm.

18 Marie Gryphon, "Giving Kids the Chaff: Finding and Keeping the Teachers We Need," Cato Policy Analysis, Sept. 25, 2006, p. 7. http://www.cato.org/pubs/pas/pa579.pdf.

19 Economic Report of the President 2006, p. 52.

20 Ibid., p. 50.

21 These numbers are my computations from Bureau of Labor Statistics data. The BLS altered its definitions and methods slightly in 2004, but the 2000 and 2006 figures remain roughly comparable.

22 Federal Reserve Survey of Consumer Finances 2004. http://www.federalreserve.gov/pubs/oss/oss2/2004/bull0206.pdf. For middle-1980s figure, see Federal Reserve Survey of Consumer Finances 1989. http://www.federalreserve.gov/pubs/oss/oss2/89/scf89home.html.

23 Kaiser Family Foundation. "Employer Health Benefits 2006," pp. 78–81. www.leff.org/insurance/7527/upload/7527.pdf.

24 Pew Research Center for the People and the Press, "Bush a Drag on Republican Midterm Prospects," Feb. 9, 2006. http://people-press.org/reports/display.php3?ReportID=270.

25 Will Lester, "In a Surprising Shift, Gore Says He Favors Single-Payer Health System," Associated Press, Nov. 15, 2002.

26 As of the summer of 2007, HR 676, the Conyers-Kucinich bill proposing a single-payer health system had attracted seventy-five cosponsors, all Democrats.

27 See, for example, Paul Krugman, "Pride, Prejudice, Ignorance," *New York Times* (Nov. 7, 2005).

28 "UAW Convention Resolves to Fight for Single Payer Health Care," July 1, 2006. http://www.healthcare-now.org/showstory.php?nid=280.

29 World Health Organization, "World Health Statistics 2006." http://www3.who.int/whosis/core/core_select_process.cfm?countries=all&indicators=nha.

30 Council for Affordable Health Insurance, "Health Insurance Mandates in the States, 2006." http://www.cahi.org/cahi_contents/resources/pdf/MandatePub2006.pdf#search=%22health%20insurance%20mandates%20in%20the%20states%202006%22.

31 See, for example, Paul Krugman, "A Serious Drug Problem," *New York Times* (May 6, 2005). http://www.pkarchive.org/column/050605.html.

32 James Bartholomew, "Die in Britain, Live in the United States," *The Spectator,* Feb. 16, 2005, p. 25.

33 Spiegel Online, "Germany's Poor Doctors." http://www.spiegel.de/international/0,1518,grossbild-575805-399537,00.html.

34 Annette Tuffs, "German Doctors Shun Eastern States," *British Medical Journal,* Oct. 25, 2003. http://www.pubmedcentral.nih.gov/articlerender.fcgi?artid=1140340.

35 Here, for example, is Sen. Dick Durbin of Illinois: "Illinois seniors wanted a Medicare benefit that would lower their drug prices. What they have today is a confusing benefit, a law that prohibits Medicare from negotiating with pharmaceutical companies and a plan that guarantees drug companies billions of dollars in profits. Medicare Part D is a reward for drug companies and a disaster for America's seniors." Press Release, Feb. 15, 2006. http://www.democraticleader.house.gov/press/releases.cfm?pressReleaseID=1422.

36 Jim Gilbert and Paul Rosenberg, "There's No Such Thing as a Free Drug," *Wall Street Journal* (April 19, 2004). http://www.bain.com/bainweb/publications/publications_detail.asp?id=16285&menu_url=publications_overview.asp.

37 Ibid.

38 National Health Policy Forum, "The Fundamentals of Community Health Centers" (Aug. 31, 2004). http://www.communityclinics.org/files/848_file_NHPF_CHC_Fundamentals.pdf#search=%22community%20health%20clinics%22.

39 Devon M. Herrick, "Uninsured by Choice," National Center for Policy Analysis, Brief No. 460, Oct. 7, 2003. http://www.ncpa.org/pub/ba/ba460/.

40 Kaiser Commission on Medicaid and the Uninsured, "The Uninsured: A Primer: Key Facts About Americans Without Health Insurance," January 2006, p. 8. http://www.kff.org/uninsured/upload/7451.pdf.

41 Centers for Medicare and Medicaid Services, "Medicare Drug Costs Drop Substantially," Feb. 2, 2006. http://www.cms.hhs.gov/apps/media/press/release.asp?Counter=1766.

42 David Gratzer, *The Cure: How Capitalism Can Save American Medicine* (Encounter, 2006), p. 1.

43 RAND Institute, "Obesity and Disability: The Shape of Things to Come," 2007. http://www.rand.org/pubs/research_briefs/2007/RAND_RB9043-1.pdf.

44 In constant 2005 dollars, the states and the federal government together spent $61.7 billion on Medicaid in 1980 and $311 billion in 2005.

45 Federal Reserve Survey of Consumer Finances 2004. http://www.federalreserve.gov/pubs/oss/oss2/2004/bull0206.pdf. For middle-1980s figure, see Federal Reserve Survey of Consumer Finances 1989. http://www.federalreserve.gov/pubs/oss/oss2/89/scf89home.html.

46 Anthony Trollope, *Phineas Finn* (Oxford, 1992), p. 341.

Five **Goal Two: Keep China Number Two**

1 See this seemingly authoritative leaked redaction of Robert Rubin's Dec. 6 meeting with the House Democratic caucus: David Sirota, "Rubin Grilled by Dems Today About Wall Street Happy Talk." http://www.workingforchange.com/blog/index.cfm?mode=entry&entry=592307CF-E0C3-F084-DA10CFAEFC6EE72B.

2 Laurence J. Kotlikoff, "Is the United States Bankrupt?" *Federal Bank of St. Louis Review,* July/August 2006, p. 239. http://research.stlouisfed.org/publications/review/06/07/Kotlikoff.pdf#search=%22kotlikoff%20bankrupt%22.

3 James Horney, "Repealing the Alternative Minimum Tax Without Offsetting the Cost Would Add $1.2 Trillion to the Federal Debt Over the Next Decade," Center for Budget and Policy Priorities, June 9, 2005. http://www.cbpp.org/6-9-05tax.htm. The Center is a liberal group whose budget projections are generally well regarded. This paper makes the interesting point that because of the way the AMT interacts with other taxes, extension of the Bush tax cuts beyond their 2010 expiration date would add an additional $179 billion to the fiscal cost of repeal, not counting the extra interest payments on the additional federal debt.

4 Report of the President's Advisory Panel on Federal Tax Reform, *Simple, Fair, and Pro-Growth: Proposals to Fix America's Tax System,* p. 190. http://www.taxreformpanel.gov/final-report/TaxReform_Ch7.pdf.

5 See Bruce Bartlett, *Imposter: How George Bush Bankrupted America and Betrayed the Reagan Legacy* (Doubleday, 2006).

6 David Bradford, *Untangling the Income Tax* (Harvard University Press, 1986).

7   Dean M. Maki and Michael G. Palumbo, "Disentangling the Wealth Effect: A Cohort Analysis of Household Savings in the 1990s," p. 32. http://www.federalreserve.gov/pubs/feds/2001/200121/200121pap.pdf.

8   Edward Gresser, "Toughest on the Poor: America's Flawed Tariff System," *Foreign Affairs,* Sept./Oct. 2002. http://www.foreignaffairs. org/20021101facomment9988/edward-gresser/toughest-on-the-poor-america-s-flawed-tariff-system.html.

9   Daniel Griswold, Stephen Slivinski, and Christopher Preble, "Six Reasons to Kill Farm Subsidies and Trade Barriers," Cato Institute, Feb. 1, 2006. http://www.freetrade.org/node/493.

10 "Cultivating Poverty: The Impact of US Cotton Subsidies on Africa," Oxfam Briefing Paper 30, 2002. http://www.oxfam.org.uk/what_ we_do/issues/trade/downloads/bp30_cotton.pdf.

11 Michael Grunwald, "Programation," *The New Republic,* Aug. 14–21, 2006, p. 33.

12 The two principal international comparison surveys, the OECD's "Program for International Assessment" and the Department of Education's "Trends in International Mathematics and Science Study," can be found at www. nces.ed.gov, the Web site of the National Center for Education Statistics.

13 Gary W. Phillips, "The Condition of Education, 2000," June 1, 2000. http://nces.ed.gov/whatsnew/commissioner/remarks2000/6_01_ 2000.asp.

14 Program for International Student Assessments 2003. http://nces.ed. gov/surveys/pisa/pisa2003highlightsfigures.asp?Quest=1&Figure=5.

15 Ibid.

16 *The Journal of Blacks in Higher Education,* "A Large Black White Scoring Gap Persists in SAT," Jan. 31, 2007. http://www.jbhe.com/features/53_ SAT.html.

17 Steven A. Camarota, "The Slowing Progress of Immigrants: An Examination of Income, Home Ownership, and Citizenship, 1970–2000," Center for Immigration Studies, March 2001. http://www.cis.org/ articles/2001/back401.html.

18 Steven A. Camarota, "Immigration from Mexico: Assessing the Impact on the United States," March 2001. http://www.cis.org/articles/ 2001/mexico/mexico.pdf.

19 George J. Borjas, "The Economic Benefits from Immigration," *Journal of Economic Perspectives,* Vol. 9, No. 2, Spring, 1995, pp. 3–22.

20 Jack Martin and Ira Mehlman, "The Cost of Illegal Immigration to

Californians," Federation for American Immigration Reform, November 2004. http://www.fairus.org/site/DocServer/ca_costs.pdf?docID=141.

21 See the forthcoming book by George J. Borjas, *Mexican Immigration to the United States* (University of Chicago Press, 2007).

22 National Center for Educational Statistics, "District Math Results by Race/Ethnicity." http://nces.ed.gov/nationsreportcard/nrc/tuda_reading_mathematics_2005/t0019.asp?subtab_id=Tab_6&tab_id=tab1&printver=Y.

23 Jay P. Greene, "High School Graduation Rates in the United States," Manhattan Institute, April 2002. http://www.manhattan-institute.org/html/cr_baeo.htm.

24 Heather MacDonald, "Hispanic Family Values," *City Journal* (Autumn 2006). http://www.city-journal.org/html/16_4_hispanic_family_values.html.

25 Steve Farkas, Ann Duffett, and Jean Johnson with Leslie Moye and Jackie Vine, "Now That I'm Here: What America's Immigrants Have to Say About Life in the U.S. Today," *Public Agenda,* January 2003. http://www.publicagenda.org/specials/immigration/immigration4.htm.

26 National Center for Educational Statistics, "Trends in Average Reading Scale Scores by Race/Ethnicity: White-Hispanic Gap." http://nces.ed.gov/nationsreportcard/ltt/results2004/sub_reading_race2.asp.

27 John D. Kasarda and James H. Johnson Jr., "The Economic Impact of the Hispanic Population on the State of North Carolina," Kenan Institute of Free Enterprise, University of North Carolina, January 2006. http://www.kenan-flagler.unc.edu/ki/reports/2006_HispanicStudy/.

28 Marti Maguire, "Illegal Immigration: Who Profits, Who Pays: Part 2, Schools Bear Burden of Immigration," *Charlotte News Observer,* Feb. 27, 2006. http://www.newsobserver.com/1155/story/412207-p2.html.

29 Tom Shuford, "Immigration and Schools, Part 2," Oct. 18, 2004, EducationNews.org. http://www.educationnews.org/writers/tom/immigration-and-schools-part-2.htm.

30 Information Office of the State Council of the People's Republic of China, "China's Employment Situation and Policies," April 2004. http://www.china.org.cn/e-white/20040426/index.htm.

31 Educational Testing Service, "America's Perfect Storm: Three Forces Changing Our Nation's Future," Feb. 5, 2007, p. 4. http://www.ets.org/Media/Education_Topics/pdf/AmericasPerfectStorm.pdf.

32 Peter Wallstein, "Quotas Foes Will Fight in Florida," *St. Petersburg Times,* March 14, 1999, http://www.sptimes.com/News/31499/State/Quotas_foe_will_fight.html.

33 "President Bush Celebrates Hispanic Heritage Day at the White House," Oct. 6, 2001. http://www.whitehouse.gov/news/releases/2006/10/20061006-12.html.

34 The 2004 exit polls purported to show Bush winning an impressive 44 percent of the Hispanic vote. Those polls were almost certainly wrong. State-by-state exit polls showed Bush winning between 25 percent and 35 percent of the Hispanic vote in almost every state of the Union, doing especially badly among Mexican-American voters in California. Bush's national average was inflated by two big scores: 55 percent among Florida Hispanics and 59 percent in Texas.

The Florida number makes sense. Florida's large Cuban-American population had voted overwhelmingly Republican for decades. Time, though, had thinned the population of refugees from Castroism, and new migration has steadily diminished the Cubans' onetime predominance: The Republican victory among Florida Hispanics almost certainly represented the end of an old story, not the launch of a new one.

Ordinary math proved, however, that the Texas count could not be right. As Ruy Tuxeira observed in his Emerging Democratic Majority weblog:

> [The exit polls show] Bush with an astonishing 59 percent of the Hispanic vote. That's an increase of 16 points in Bush's support over 2000 and a shift in margin of 29 points (from an 11-point deficit to an 18-point lead).
>
> The poll also claims that this mega-shift happened at the same time that Bush's support was being *compressed* among whites. Bush's support, the exit poll claims, dropped by a point among Texas whites compared to 2000, at the same time as Kerry's support among Texas whites rose by 4 points compared to Gore's. So Texas's favorite son runs for reelection and widens his margin among white voters practically everywhere—except Texas, where he loses ground! But among Hispanics in Texas, he gets a massive 29-point shift in his favor.

This pattern just doesn't make sense. But where the Texas poll makes the least sense of all is when you try to match them up with the county-level voting returns. If Bush was pulling over 70 percent of the white vote and almost 60 percent of the Hispanic vote, how on earth did he lose *any* counties in Texas?

http://www.emergingdemocraticmajorityweblog.com/donkeyrising/archives/000951.php.

In fact, Bush lost Hispanic-majority counties all over south Texas—which would imply (if the poll is correct) that he racked up even huger 70 percent supermajorities among Hispanics in urban Texas—and that just defies common sense. The 59 percent number for Bush's support among Texas Hispanics has to be wrong, and the 44 percent national figure therefore has to be wrong as well.

35 MacDonald, op. cit.

36 Statement of Sen. John McCain Before the Senate Judiciary Committee, July 26, 2005. http://mccain.senate.gov/press_office/view_article.cfm?id=149.

37 The Bureau of Labor Statistics estimates that there are 50–60 million total new hires each year. Multiplied by 5 percent, that translates into 2.5 million to 3 million illegal-alien hires.

38 Jessica Vaughan, "Attrition Through Enforcement: A Cost-Effective Strategy to Shrink the Illegal Population," Center for Immigration Studies, April 2006. http://www.cis.org/articles/2006/back406.html.

39 See, for example, Kevin Milligan, "Subsidizing the Stork: New Evidence on Tax Incentives and Fertility," March 2002. http://www.nber.org/papers/8845.

40 See, for example, Isaac Ehrlich, Jinyoung Kim, "Has Social Security Influenced Family Formation and Fertility in OECD Countries? An Economic and Econometric Analysis." http://www.nber.org/papers/w12869.

Six Goal Three: New Life for the Pro-Life

1 NBC News/*Wall Street Journal* poll, June 25–28, 2004. http://www.pollingreport.com/science.htm.

2 The ad can be seen on YouTube at http://www.youtube.com/watch?v=a9WB_PXjTBo.

3   Missouri voters did, however, elect a dead Democrat in 2000. That
    year, Governor Mel Carnahan challenged incumbent senator John
    Ashcroft. Carnahan, his son Randy, and a campaign aide died in a
    plane crash three weeks before voting day. Missouri law did not allow
    for a change of candidate so close to the election, so Carnahan's name
    remained on the ballot. Out of respect for the deceased, incumbent
    John Ashcroft suspended his campaign. The Democrats won, and Act-
    ing Governor Roger Wilson appointed Carnahan's widow, Jeane, to
    fill his place until a special election could be held in 2002. Jim Talent
    then recovered the seat for the GOP.

4   ABC News/Beliefnet poll, June 26, 2001. http://www.abcnews.go.
    com/sections/politics/DailyNews/poll010626.html.

5   American RadioWorks, "The Fertility Race," Sept. 20, 1999. http://
    americanradioworks.publicradio.org/features/fertility_race/part4/
    section3.shtml.

6   Shannon Brownlee, "Designer Babies," *Washington Monthly,* March 2002.
    http://www.washingtonmonthly.com/features/2001/0203.brownlee.
    html.

7   Andrew Kohut, "A Political Victory That Wasn't," *New York Times,*
    March 23, 2005. http://www.nytimes.com/2005/03/23/opinion/23
    Kohut.html?ex=1269234000&en=8309fe1397c4d8b6&ei=5090&partner
    =rssuserland.

8   http://www.vatican.va/holy_father/john_paul_ii/encyclicals/docu-
    ments/hf_jp-ii_enc_25031995_evangelium-vitae_en.html.

9   Ramesh Ponnuru, "Not Dead Yet," *National Review,* May 17, 1999,
    www.nationalreview.com/17may99/ponnuru051799.html.

10 NARAL-ProChoice America Foundation, "*Roe v. Wade* and the
    Right to Choose," Jan. 24, 2006. http://www.prochoiceamerica.org/
    assets/files/CourtsSCOTUS-Roe.pdf.

11 Jonathan Finer, "Kerry Says He Believes Life Starts at Conception,"
    Washington Post, July 5, 2004, p. A06. http://www.washingtonpost.
    com/wpdyn/articles/A27920-2004Jul4.html.

12 Remarks by Senator Clinton to New York State Family Planners,
    Jan. 24, 2005. http://clinton.senate.gov/~clinton/speeches/2005125A05.
    html.

13 Guttmacher Institute, "Facts on Induced Abortion in the United
    States," May 2006. http://www.guttmacher.org/pubs/fb_induced_
    abortion.html.

14 Guttmacher Institute, "An Overview of Abortion in the United

States," June 2005. http://www.guttmacher.org/media/presskits/2005/06/28/abortionoverview.html.

15 For a summary and list of these polls, see, for example, Wanda Franz, "Productive Pro-Life Work," *National Right to Life News,* June 2007. http://www.nrlc.org/news/2007/NRL07/PresidentColumn.html.

16 Norval D. Glenn, "With This Ring: A National Survey on Marriage in America," National Fatherhood Initiative 2005, p. 8. http://www.fatherhood.org/doclibrary/nms.pdf.

17 Steven P. Martin "Trends in Marital Dissolution by Women's Education in the United States," Demographic Research, Vol. 15, Article 20, Dec. 13, 2006. http://www.demographic-research.org/volumes/vol15/20/15-20.pdf.

18 Kaiser Family Foundation, "US Teen Sexual Activity," January 2005. http://www.kff.org/youthhivstds/upload/U-S-Teen-Sexual-Activity-Fact-Sheet.pdf.

19 Martin, op. cit.

20 Kay Hymowitz, "Marriage and Caste in America," *City Journal* (Winter 2006). http://www.city-journal.org/html/16_1_marriage_gap.html.

21 Ibid.

22 Robert I. Lerman, "How Do Marriage, Cohabitation, and Single Parenthood Affect the Material Hardships of Families with Children?" Urban Institute, July 2002. http://www.urban.org/UploadedPDF/410539_SippPaper.pdf. See especially pp. 20–22.

23 Sara McLanahan and Gary Sandefur, *Growing Up With a Single Parent: What Hurts, What Helps* (Harvard University Press, 1994), pp. 40–42.

24 Ibid., pp. 45–46.

25 Ibid., pp. 46–48.

26 Ibid., pp. 48–49.

27 Ibid., pp. 52–54.

28 Ibid., p. 153.

29 Hymowitz, op. cit.

30 National Fatherhood Initiative, "With This Ring: A National Survey on Marriage in America," p. 7. http://www.fatherhood.org/doclibrary/nms.pdf.

31 Maggie Gallagher, "Closing the Divorce Divide," Nov. 30, 2005. Institute for Marriage and Public Policy. http://www.marriagedebate.com/2005/11/closing-divorce-dividemaggie-gallagher.htm.

32 See Maggie Gallagher, "Everything You Always Wanted to Know About Marriage," National Review Online, Feb. 23, 2006. http://

www.nationalreview.com/comment/gallagher200602230759.asp Gallagher cited the UCLA National Survey of Freshmen, which found 42 percent of 2,000 freshmen agreed with the statement: "If two people really like each other, it's all right for them to have sex even if they have known each other for only a very short time." In 1980, 48 percent of freshmen had agreed with that statement.

33 *Statistics Netherlands,* Key Figures: Marriage and Partnership Registrations. http://statline.cbs.nl/StatWeb/table.asp?PA=37772eng&D1=0-28,35-47&D2=(l-11)-l&DM=SLEN&LA=en&TT=2.

34 *Statistical Yearbook of Norway 2006,* Table 97: Partnerships Contracted. http://www.ssb.no/english/yearbook/tab/tab-097.html.

35 Maggie Gallagher and Joshua Baker, "Same-Sex Unions and Divorce Risk: Evidence from Sweden," May 3, 2004. http://www.marriagedebate.com/pdf/SSdivorcerisk.pdf.

36 David Blankenhorn, "Defining Marriage Down," *Weekly Standard,* April 2, 2007. http://www.weeklystandard.com/Content/Public/Articles/000/000/013/451Noxve.asp.

37 Simon Jackman, "Same-Sex Marriage Ballot Initiatives and Conservative Mobilization in the 2004 Election." http://jackman.stanford.edu/papers/RISSPresentation.pdf.

The states where Bush's vote rose most were: Hawaii, Rhode Island, New Jersey, Alabama, and Tennessee. The states where his vote rose least: Vermont, South Dakota (in those two, his share of the vote actually declined), North Carolina, the District of Columbia, Montana,★ Oregon,★ New Hampshire, Nevada, Maine, and Ohio.★

The asterisked states had same-sex-marriage initiatives on their ballots.

38 The Ad Council, "Second Hand Smoke and Kids." http://www.adcouncil.org/default.aspx?id=58.

39 Eli Lehrer, "The Most Silent Crime," National Review Online, April 29, 2003. http://www.nationalreview.com/comment/comment-lehrer042903.asp.

Seven Goal Four: Green Conservatism

1 Harris Poll 77, Oct. 13, 2005. http://www.harrisinteractive.com/harris_poll/index.asp?PID=607.

2 Nancy Stauffer, "MIT Survey: Climate Change Tops List of Americans' Concerns," Nov. 1, 2006. http://web.mit.edu/newsoffice/2006/survey.html.

3 Environment News Service, "Poll: Why Pro-Environmental Voters Fail to Vote for Environment," Sept. 20, 2005. http://www.ens-news-wire.com/ens/sep2005/2005-09-20-03.asp.

4 National Center for Research on Women, "Women's Priorities 2006," Nov. 2, 2006. http://www.ncrw.org/researchforaction/PollExecSummary.htm.

5 Pew Research Center for the People and the Press, "Young Americans and Women Less Informed," Dec. 28, 1995. http://people-press.org/reports/display.php3?ReportID=134.

6 CBS/MTV/NYT poll, June 26, 2007. http://www.cbsnews.com/stories/2007/06/26/opinion/polls/main2983410.shtml.

7 Pew Research Center for the People and the Press, "Economic Pessimism Grows, Gas Prices Pinch," Sept. 15, 2005. http://people-press.org/reports/display.php3?ReportID=257.

8 Edmunds.com, "The Real Costs of Owning a Hybrid." http://www.edmunds.com/advice/fueleconomy/articles/103708/article.html.

9 Robert Gilman, "Energy Update: Some Surprising Developments in Power Supply and Demand, an Interview with Amory B. Lovins." *In Context: A Quarterly of Humane Sustainable Culture* 14, August 1986, p. 27. http://www.context.org/ICLIB/IC14/ALovins.htm.

10 Peter Huber and Mark Mills, "Got a Computer? More Power to You," *Wall Street Journal,* Sept. 6, 2000. http://www.manhattan-institute.org/html/_wsj-got_a_comp.htm.

11 Nancy Pelosi, "Energy Bill Is a Missed Opportunity," July 28, 2005. http://www.house.gov/pelosi/press/releases/July05/energy.html.

12 Eugene Trisko, "Energy Cost Impacts on American Families," BalancedEnergy.org, May 2007, p. 8. http://www.ceednet.org/docs/ABEC%20Media%20Room%20Docs/ABEC%20Energy%20Costs%201997%20to%202007%20507-2.pdf.

13 Bjorn Lomborg, "Perspective on Climate Change," Testimony to the House Science and Technology Committee and Senate Environment and Public Works Committee, Mar. 21, 2007. http://www.copenhagenconsensus.com/Admin/Public/DWSDownload.aspx?File=Files%2FFiler%2FBjorn%2FPerspective_on_Climate_Change_Lomborg_Final.pdf.

14 Victor Yasmann, "Russia: Reviving the Army, Revising Military Doctrine," Radio Liberty, http://www.rferl.org/featuresarticle/2007/03/63173250-a8b3-40d0-a26d-219ed25d91b2.html.

15 Gustavo Coronel, "Corruption, Mismanagement, and Abuse of Power

in Hugo Chavez's Venezuela," Cato Institute, Nov. 27, 2006, p. 6. http://www.cato.org/pubs/dpa/dpa2.pdf.

16 Robert Freedman, "Feeling the Pinch," *Realtor Magazine,* Aug. 1, 2006. http://www.realtor.org/rmomag.nsf/pages/FrontLinesledeaug06.

17 Mining Health and Safety Administration data gathered at http://www. msha.gov/STATS/PART50/WQ/2006/table1.pdf and http://www. msha.gov/STATS/PART50/WQ/2006/table5.pdf. Note that Table 1 refers to operators and Table 5 refers to contractors, so that the two have to be added together to produce a grand total for killed and injured.

18 The Department of Energy is required by law to produce an annual report on U.S. greenhouse gas emissions. The report for 2005 can be read at ftp://ftp.eia.doe.gov/pub/oiaf/1605/cdrom/pdf/ggrpt/057305. pdf.

19 U.S. Department of Energy, "Indicators of Energy Efficiency in the United States." http://intensityindicators.pnl.gov/total_highlights.stm.

20 See, for example, this speech from June 15, 2005, at http://www.white-house.gov/news/releases/2005/06/20050615-2.html.

21 Al Gore, *Earth in the Balance: Ecology and the Human Spirit* (Houghton Mifflin, 1992), p. 219.

22 Gore, *Earth in the Balance,* pp. 220–21.

23 Andrew Coyne, "Outfoxing Dion on his own Green Turf," *The National Post,* Feb. 21, 2007. http://andrewcoyne.com/columns/2007/02/ outfoxing-dion-on-his-own-green-turf.php.

24 Gregg Easterbrook, *The Progress Paradox: How Life Gets Better While People Feel Worse* (Random House, 2003), p. 43.

Eight Goal Five: Win the War on Terror

1 John DiStaso, "Bush: Stay the course on Iraq," *Manchester Union Leader,* Sept. 18, 2004, p. A1.

2 ABC News/*Washington Post* poll, http://www.pollingreport.com/ iraq.htm.

3 Andrea Elliott, "More Muslims Are Coming to US After a Decline in Wake of 9/11," *New York Times,* Sept. 10, 2006. http://select.nytimes. com/search/restricted/article?res=F1081FFB3F550C738DDDA00894 DE404482.

4 Department of Homeland Security, "Immigration Enforcement Actions 2005," November 2006. http://www.dhs.gov/xlibrary/assets/ statistics/yearbook/2005/Enforcement_AR_05.pdf.

5   The Pew Research Center for People and the Press, "Views of Islam Remain Sharply Divided." http://people-press.org/commentary/display.php3?AnalysisID=96.

6   The Pew Research Center for People and the Press, "Post-9/11 Attitudes." http://pewforum.org/publications/surveys/post911poll.pdf.

7   Zogby International, "The Ten Nation 'Impressions of America' Poll," April 11, 2002. http://www.zogby.com/features/features.dbm?ID=141.

8   Memri.org, "Terror in America (8)," Sept. 21, 2001, Special Dispatch 274.

9   Pew Research Center for the People and the Press, "Muslim Americans: Middle Class and Mostly Mainstream," May 22, 2007. http://people-press.org/reports/display.php3?ReportID=329

10 Memri.org, "Terror in America (10)," Sept. 25, 2001, Special Dispatch 277.

11 Pew Research Center for the People and the Press, "Muslims in Europe," July 6, 2006. http://pewresearch.org/pubs/232/muslims-in-europe.

12 Ibid.

13 Peter Riddell, "Poll Shows Voters Believe Press Is Right Not to Publish Cartoons," *The Times,* Feb. 7, 2006. http://www.timesonline.co.uk/tol/news/politics/article727952.ece.

14 Ibid.

15 Claudia Deane and Darryl Fears, "Negative Views of Islam Increasing," *Washington Post,* March 9, 2006. http://www.washingtonpost.com/wp-dyn/content/article/2006/03/08/AR2006030802221.html.

16 *USA Today*/CNN/Gallup poll, Feb. 13, 2006. http://www.usatoday.com/news/washington/2006-02-13-usat-poll_x.htm.

17 Those interested in my views on this question can see the book I co-authored with Richard Perle, *An End to Evil: How to Win the War on Terror* (Random House, 2004).

18 Al Gore, "Remarks for UN Security Council Session on AIDS in Africa," Jan. 10, 2000. http://clinton3.nara.gov/WH/EOP/OVP/speeches/unaid_health.html.

19 Bill Clinton, Remarks to 2004 Democratic Convention. http://www.cnn.com/2004/ALLPOLITICS/07/26/dems.clinton.transcript/.

20 *The Empty Cradle,* p. 63.

21 Robert J. Shapiro, "Democracy in America," presented to the Engelsberg Seminar, June 15, 2007, adapted from the book *Futurecast: How Three Great Forces Will Change the Way We Live* (St. Martin's Press, 2008).

22 At the time of Partition in 1947, Kashmir was a Muslim-majority territory ruled by a Hindu prince. The prince supposedly acceded to India, but under circumstances that gave rise to strong suspicions of coercion and fraud. India and Pakistan came to blows over Kashmir in 1948. India ended the war in control of the most populous and valuable area of Kashmir. Under the terms of the 1949 UN-sponsored cease-fire, India was to have held a referendum to allow Kashmiris to decide for themselves whether to join Pakistan. India has never done so. An insurgency erupted in Kashmir in the 1990s, possibly instigated by and certainly supported by Pakistan. India has used brutal methods to suppress the uprising. The unsuccessful insurgents have come under the influence of al Qaeda–style Islamists and have increasingly resorted to terrorist violence in Indian cities.

23 http://usinfo.state.gov/xarchives/display.html?p=washfile-english& y=2006&m=March&x=20060303085507eaifaso.6019403.

24 Deutsche Bank Research, "China and India: A Visual Essay," Oct. 10, 2005. http://www.dbresearch.com/PROD/DBR_INTERNET_DE-PROD/PROD0000000000192108.pdf.

25 *An End to Evil*, pp. 38–39.

26 Shawn Donnen, "Little Clarity on How Aid Gets Spent," *Financial Times,* December 23, 2005, p. 8.

27 Andrew Kohut, "Bush's Concern Over Isolationism Reflects More than Just Rhetoric," Pew Research Center for the People and the Press, Feb. 3, 2006. http://pewresearch.org/obdeck/?ObDeckID=3.

28 This is not hindsight wisdom on my part. I made this point often in 2003–2004—for example, in an article for the *Wall Street Journal* of Nov. 12, 2004, "A New Style for a New Mandate," http://www.davidfrum.com/archive_article.asp?YEAR=2004&ID=192.

On 9/11, the United States was plunged into a new era for which it was radically unprepared. Ever since, the U.S. government has been improvising as it goes. Sometimes the improvisation has been very successful, as it was with the new military tactics used in the Afghan campaign. Sometimes the improvisation has led us into real trouble—as the lack of clear and accepted rules for the treatment of captured terrorists did at Abu Ghraib. Americans have a big job of institution-building and rule-writing ahead of them. Writing these rules deep inside the administration and then applying them at the discretion of the executive practically invites the courts to review and rewrite them—a job that courts are not well suited to do. Much of the Patriot Act expires next year. It would be a terrible thing for the whole country if a successor law ended up being enacted on a party-line vote.

President Bush should be convening national commissions that include respected Democratic lawyers and elected officials—people like former solicitor general Walter Dellinger—to propose a comprehensive set of laws and rules to govern the war on terror at home and overseas.

Nine Goal Six: Rediscover Conservative Ideals

1 Based on the Center for Responsive Politics' estimate of $2.59 billion in total annual spending on lobbying the federal government.

2 Transcript available at http://www.family.org/welcome/press/a0038214.cfm.

3 John H. Fund, "Judgment Call," *Opinion Journal,* Oct. 17, 2005. http://www.opinionjournal.com/diary/?id=110007415.

4 Jo Becker, "In Speeches from 1990s, Clues About Miers' Views: Nominee Defended Social Activism," *Washington Post,* Oct. 26, 2005, p. A1.

5 Tom Humphrey, "Bush Stumps for Alexander, civics in school," *Knoxville News-Sentinel* (Sept. 18, 2002), p. B1.

6 Hugh Hewitt, "Yes, Gentlemen, I am a Party Man," Oct. 6, 2005. http://hughhewitt.com/archives/2005/10/02-week/index.php#a000319.

7 Thomas Lifson, "Don't Misunderestimate Miers," Oct. 4, 2005. http://www.americanthinker.com/articles.php?article_id=4876.

8 Marvin Olasky, "One Reason Miers' Evangelical Belief Is Important," October 5, 2005. http://www.worldmagblog.com/blog/archives/018942.html.

9 Eduardo Porter, "Katrina Begets a Baby Boom by Immigrants," *New York Times,* Dec. 11, 2006. http://www.nytimes.com/2006/12/11/us/nationalspecial/11babies.html?ex=1323493200&en=68c902d882214ed1&ei=5088&partner=rssnyt&emc=rss.

10 George Lakoff, *Don't Think of an Elephant* (Chelsea Green, 2004), p. 3.

11 See Drew Westen, *The Political Brain: The Role of Emotion in Deciding the Fate of the Nation* (Public Affairs, 2007).

ACKNOWLEDGMENTS

This book, short in length, has been long in making. I began work soon after the 2004 election in an effort to warn my fellow Republicans against the triumphalism of the moment. I finished in mid-2007, a season of conservative pessimism verging on panic.

Through much of that time, I felt like a financial writer trying to cover the 1929 crash: The bad news kept overtaking my grimmest forecasts. In 2005, it seemed a very bold prediction that the Republicans would lose both houses of Congress in 2006. By 2007, it seemed an even bolder prediction that the Grand Old Party could soon recover its losses. The book's working title through most of the writing period was *The Next Republican President.* I'd joke to friends: "It's a very long-term project."

Along the way, I've had to reconsider a lifetime of beliefs. That has not been an easy or a comfortable process, and I doubt that I could ever have completed it without the assistance of kind friends and colleagues who deserve better thanks than these too few words.

First mention has to go to the brilliant leaders and scholars of the

American Enterprise Institute. Chris DeMuth and David Gerson have given me the opportunity and the freedom to follow my thoughts, often in very unexpected directions. They have created an environment that is both supportive and challenging, and I am profoundly grateful to them for extending the hospitality of AEI to me.

The AEI spirit is best summed up by a probably apocryphal joke about Henry Kissinger and a junior NSC aide. The aide had toiled and toiled on a report for his chief. The next morning, Kissinger called him in and furiously demanded: "Is *this* your best work?" Humiliated and abashed, the aide promised to redo it. Two days pass, the work is resubmitted. This time Kissinger is even more furious. "Really, are you seriously telling me that this is the best you can do?" Shattered, crestfallen, the aide abjectly admits, "I am sorry, Dr. Kissinger, I really am, but yes this is the best I can do." "Very well," comes the answer. "In that case I will read it."

I must thank too my assistants at AEI, first Igor Khrestin, then Kara Flook. They became used to a barrage of frantic, disparate, urgent queries on everything from differentials in state Medicaid expenditures to the text of President William Henry Harrison's inaugural address—and responded to every query with speed and skill. I am a little embarrassed about how much of their labor ended up on the cutting-room floor: If all the material cut from this book were added together, it would constitute a volume longer than the one you hold in your hand.

Thanks to Jennifer Rudolph Walsh, my brilliant super-agent, who has never been more creative, more persevering, and more indispensable than she was on this extended project.

Thanks (and apologies too for all the difficulties I inflicted on them) to the superb team I dealt with at Doubleday: Bill Thomas, Dan Feder, Chris Fortunato, and my long-suffering editor, Adam Bellow, above all. Adam is living proof that there are giants in publishing still. He has shaped some of the most important books of our times, and I am honored to be numbered among his authors.

Many friends, editors, interlocuters, and e-mail correspondents have helped me refine and revise the ideas incorporated here, usually without ever knowing how helpful they had been. I want to offer special thanks to John Gardner, Newt Gingrich, Dean Godson, Toby Harshaw, Jonathan Kay, Rich Lowry, Jay Nordlinger, David Shipley, Tunku Varadarajan, Richard Yeselson, and all the participants in the political seminars at AEI's annual World Forum.

The book's ultimate title was suggested by my good friend Laura Ingraham, truly one of those rare people who is most a friend when most needed.

My father, Murray Frum, was an early and late editor, critic, and all-purpose font of ideas. My in-laws, Peter and Yvonne Worthington, once again extended the hospitality of their barn in Prince Edward County, Ontario, as a writing retreat.

I fear that this book has taught some very bad lessons to my children, Miranda, Nathaniel, and Beatrice. Nathaniel in particular would ask with all the wide-eyed sarcasm of a *South Park*-loving thirteen-year-old, "I thought the book was supposed to have been finished *last* December?" Sorry, Nat: It's only in high school that there are no extensions. For their patience with a father whose work interfered with too many weekends and vacations, I say a fervent "thanks."

As ever and always, my wife Danielle manages to be at once editor, critic, and muse. Without her, I would have thrown this book away long ago; without her, I would not be myself. The words I quoted in a book I published eleven years ago reverberate after two decades of marriage with ever profounder truth:

She is mine own,
And I as rich in having such a jewel
As twenty seas, if all their sand were pearl,
The water nectar, and the rocks pure gold.

—Washington, D.C.,
September 2007

INDEX